THE ACTS OF OBLIVION

English poet and critic Paul Batchelor's first collection of poems, *The Sinking Road*, was published in 2008. A chapbook, *The Love Darg*, was published by Clutag in 2014. He has won the *Times* Stephen Spender Prize for Translation and the Edwin Morgan International Poetry Prize. His reviews have appeared in the *New Statesman*, the *Guardian*, *Poetry*, and the *Times Literary Supplement*. He is Director of Creative Writing at Durham University.

The Acts
of Oblivion

PAUL BATCHELOR

CARCANET POETRY

First published in Great Britain in 2021 by
Carcanet/Northern House
Alliance House, 30 Cross Street
Manchester, M2 7AQ
www.carcanet.co.uk

A CIP catalogue record for this book is
available from the British Library.

ISBN 978 1 80017 199 2

Book design by Andrew Latimer
Printed in Great Britain by SRP Ltd, Exeter, Devon

The publisher acknowledges financial
assistance from Arts Council England.

CONTENTS

III. BRANTWOOD SENILIA

IV. THE MARBLE VEIL

for Frances

Acknowledgements

Ten of these poems, or earlier versions of them, appeared in a chapbook, *The Love Darg*, published by Clutag in 2014. Thanks are also due to the editors of the following anthologies:

Eddie@90: Poems for Edwin Morgan (Mariscat), *Gift: a Chapbook for Seamus Heaney* (Newcastle University), *Grand Tour: Travels through the Young Poetry in Europe* (Carl Hanser), *Identity Parade* (Bloodaxe), *Oxford New Poets 2013* (Oxford*Poets*/Carcanet), *The Best of Poetry London: Poetry and Prose 1988-2013* (Carcanet), *The Forward Book of Poetry 2014* (Forward Worldwide), *The Penguin Book of Elegy* (Penguin), and *Tokens for the Foundlings* (Seren).

Thanks also to the editors of the following publications:

Ambit, Antiphon, Blackbox Manifold, B O D Y, BBC Radio 3, *The Compass, The Edinburgh Review, Granta, Kaffeeklatsch, The London Review of Books, Manchester Review, Poetry,* the Poetry Archive, *Poetry Ireland Review, Poetry London, Poetry Review, The Rialto, Shearsman, Subtropics, The Times,* the *Times Literary Supplement,* and *Transect.*

'Comeuppance' won the 2009 Edwin Morgan International Poetry Competition. 'The Damned' won the 2009 *Times* Stephen Spender Prize for Translation.

Thanks to the Arts Council for a bursary, to the Arthur Welton Foundation for an award in 2011, to the staff at Yaddo, to Manchester University for a Writing Fellowship in 2012, and to St Cuthbert's Society, Durham University, for a residency in 2014. Thanks to Jeff Nosbaum, Alba Zeigler-Bailey, and Frances Leviston.

THE ACTS OF OBLIVION

THE REUNION
after Homer, The Odyssey, *Book XI, 197–224*

Neither disease
  nor keen-eyed Diana
with her subtle shafts
  stole upon me:

they say that life
  can waste in grief,
great sorrow drain
  heat from the blood,

and it was longing for thee —
  for our little chats
my glorious son
  for your kindnesses —

for want of these
  my long life ebbed
and sobbed away
  my son, my son…

How I longed to embrace her!
  How my heart filled
at every word —
  but she'd grow vague

and resolve like a dream
  at the touch of dawn
whenever I tried
  to draw any closer

until my pain
　　was such that I cried:
'Hug me again —
　　now as of old

we should cast our arms
　　about each other,
lament together…
　　Why won't you stay —

or are you a ghost
　　cruel Persephone
sent to torment me
　　in this House of Death?'

Unluckiest man
　　in all the world,
this is just the way
　　of things down here —

sinews can't join
　　flesh to bone
once the fire
　　of death has been at them,

once the spirit
　　has quickened and gone.
Go back now — run
　　fast as you can

back to the light
　　with all you have learned
and tell your wife
　　before you forget.

I

BROTHER COAL

And I think I have seen faces, and heard voices, by road and street side,
which claimed or conferred as much as ever the loveliest or saddest of
Camelot. As I watch them, the feeling continually weighs upon me, day
by day, more and more, that not the grief of the world but the loss of it is
the wonder of it. I see creatures so full of all power and beauty, with none
to understand or teach or save them. The making in them of miracles, and
all cast away, for ever lost as far as we can trace. And no 'in memoriam'.
— John Ruskin, letter to Tennyson, September 1859

BROTHER COAL

I

Childhood fantasies, the kind that die hard,
staged in the darkness of the coal shed;
a mother's boy knuckling down for a shift
of glamorous, imaginary graft;
the difficult one, ideas below his station,
a could-be diamond lacking in ambition —
and there you are as always, there you are,
playmate, shadow, secret sharer,
genius loci of the bunker, fast asleep
like a tramp wrapped tight in a dirty oil-cape.

II

From back-to-backs that echo with raised voices
to row against row of little, Dutch-style houses;
the rec, the tip, the cornershop, the street,
a warren of cul-de-sacs, my earthly estate —
except I never liked to play outside.
Scholarly, timid, anxious to succeed,
first chance I got I left it all behind
and then (I couldn't help myself) returned.
Sooner than I would dare admit I sensed
that this is all I stay buoyed up against.

III

My childish heart sinks like a falling flare.
Dad asks if he is making himself clear:
no pets allowed. In this house all the warmth
we can afford is right there in the hearth,
where you cringe on your haunches in the cree
or spatter awake in wet coughs and outcry.
You drowse open-eyed. You settle and resettle
as a dog curled in its basket might shift a little,
lift its muzzle to salute a ghost
and then — sigh of the disregarded — resume its rest...

IV

A black cabinet painted shut, the spellbound doors
promising untold tinctures and liqueurs —
a miser's hoard, a treasure trove cool to the touch,
though never as cold as the spent white ash
he had to rake out last thing every night
(he too was cold, he too was spent and white).
I see him on his knees as though in prayer,
huffing and puffing life into the fire;
I see him rise, the cupped flare of a match
like sudden anger. He too was quick to catch.

V

(Or, better fettled, he might mind on
how back in the day, and nowt but a bairn
and all this nowt but pits, one idea of fun
was to drag a tin bath to the smouldering crown
of a slag heap, and then toboggan down...
You'd have to watch yourself though, not to overturn:
the heat locked in the spoil could burn —
he'd seen the flesh fall clean from the bone —
and leave a scar, a glib blue stain
that'd grow with you till you were both full-grown.)

VI

Fibred, veined, fissured like an icicle —
black, pleated muscle ripped with black blood-crystal.
It stranged my mind that I could never lift
a shovelful or lug a sack — the heft!
So much unmanageable worldliness
overmatching me! — and yet a single piece
felt buoyant, quick, and easily borne.
Before such mysteries, I hunker down
in contemplation. I turn and burn
in claustral darkness. I found a church of one.

VII

And you turn too, you dream on, bide & deepen
while forests rise & fall, you wait to happen,
and then — you begin to slip from hand to hand
bestowing crumbs of soot, a never-spent
fortune passing down intact
through generations, from the men you wrecked
to the sons raised in their image, all of them joined
in dream reunions underground
by the scab who turns, cribbed in the sweat of his bed,
to face the wall and visit the land of Nod.

VIII

Implicit as the fault in a flawed prism
or the seamless ambiguity of a poem,
your darker promise: to give nothing away.
To make us pay for everything. To someday
run out on us, that we might balance the cost
of losing you against all that was lost
when you were found hung in your galleries,
entombed within yourself, far from the sun's rays —
a fluted curtain no wind stirs;
sails of wet leather, a black ship in black waters;

IX

wet as a tooth, enamelled like a tooth
that flinches from the pick; an estuary of earth
squandering yourself, prodigal as rain
on the just and unjust until both lie prone;
burnt amber honey with comb of burnt quartz,
warm as a wintering hive, back-lit with glints;
Isaiah's emblem; envious shadow thrown
under the world; inestimable stone
bought at a price; unmournable as time
and, like anything unmournable, sublime.

X

Compacted sentiment, this pseudo-factual,
homely, far-fetched stuff. O, Brother Coal,
shine your black torch on such complacency
for shame! Shine your black torch that I may see
each brush-off, cave-in and betrayal
implicated in your comet's tail.
O, stardust of disasters and diseases,
child labour, roof collapse and silicosis,
let me stand face to face with your dark mirror
until the shadows glitter and grow clear.

( )

(kiroop sweep)   (pet lin)   (loop the loop)

(dip wheat)   (dew lop)   (teeter flip)

(pew slip)

(lea plut)   (pewter pip)

(lap wite)

(tchew leap)

(acute sleep)

(be whisht)

(peesweep)

(tup-heidit)

(keep toot)

(swoop a bit)

(peez-weep)

(peewit)   (peewit)   (peewit)

PIT PONIES

But what is that clinking in the darkness?
Louis MacNeice

Listen. They're singing in your other life:
'Faith of our Fathers' sounding clear as day
from the pit-head where half the village has turned out
to hear the latest news from underground,
news that will be brought to them by the caged ponies
hauled up and loosed in Raff Smith's field.

Could that have been you in Raff Smith's field,
mouthing the words and listening to the cages lift,
watching sunlight break on dirty ponies,
noting the way, unshoed for their big day,
each one flinches on the treacherous ground,
pauses and sniffs, then rears and blunders about?

As at a starting pistol they gallop out
and a roll of thunder takes hold of the field —
thunder, or else an endless round
of cannon fire. Hooves plunge and lift.
They pitch themselves headlong into the day:
runty, fabulously stubborn pit ponies.

But they seem to have a sense, the ponies,
a sidelong kind of sense about
getting called in at last light on the fifth day:
they seem to know the strike has failed,
as though they felt the tug of their old lives.
They shy and shake their heads. They paw the ground.

Let's leave them there for now, holding their ground
for all it's worth, and say the ponies
might maintain their stand-off, as the livid
shades of miners might yet stagger out
of history into the pitched field
dotted with cannonballs you see today.

Let's pretend you might come back some day
to wait a lifetime on this scrap of ground
until the silence — like the silence of a field
after battle — breaks, and you hear ponies
buck and whinny as the chains pay out
and once again the rusty cages lift...

As though the day was won, as though the ground
was given, the ponies gallop out
to claim their piece of field, their only life.

RETURNS

I   *In Keenleysides DIY*

Sun-warmed copper and the dull shine of the stepladder.
Nails arranged by size in drawers. A masculine dream of order.
Cut pine: measured, seasoned, expectant; the smell smart as a whip,
quick as the clip you got for back-chat. Pallets. Bolt cutters.
A buck-toothed fork-lift truck. An endless row of coloured doors
opening on to nothing but more doors. A pyramid of tins that rise
like the wish to cry. Come-heres. But-whys. *Come-heres.* What-fors.
And look at you now, making yourself look childish.

II   *In Gleghorn's Sweet Shop*

A Coronation mug & tea towel. A Rangers scarf nailed to the wall.
The rustle of brown paper and, behind the counter's sentry box,
Old Gleghorn shuffling back & forth, boss-eyed, ambassadorial
in his navy-blue reefer jacket, tie pin, brass buttons and hair oil.
He counts out Black Jacks while you browse racks of flyblown comics
that curl their lips at you: redcoats with swagger sticks;
Nazis tunnelling under Buck House. Bullets. Brittle.
Bottles of battery acid the colour of orange pop.

III   *In M&M Fashions*

Those plastic guns that came with spools of thin red paper ribbon
peppered with caps that went off with a crack & left a tang of tin,
a prickle of smoke, a smack just like that trick where someone — it
would be your dad — would squeeze a belt into a figure *8* then tug it tight:
a fierce snap; yet you could hold your hand inside & no harm done —
those made-in-Taiwan guns you'd get in last-chance boutiques run
by someone's mam — the sort who did an evening class & got divorced —
baskets of cheap tat by the till. Once they're gone they're gone though but.

IV   *In the street*

A birdshit-badged memorial to the local-lad-done-good
footballing legend, and beneath it, dead to the world,
Guy Fawkes in a crimson shell-suit & self-inflicted haircut.
A bag of glue. A backward stare — blank as a borstal dot,
unreturnable. His lot. Your lot. From a billboard high
above it all, Leah Betts beams down her tragic tagline (*Sorted*)
and everywhere the unforgivable daughters of the poor
totter home on mock-fashionable shoes.

A BRACE OF SNIPE

The point
I'm coming back to
is the time Oz told me —
we were sat in the kitchen, having a bit craic
while Mam sat with Tina,
watching her smoke —

told me while he, too, lit up,
for he liked a smoke himself, though his manner
in so doing was distinct: he drank deep
while Tina'd sip
pent little sighs,
eyes on everything but you —

told me & Gav,
because Gav would be there too,
'the bairn', it being our custom to split
the cramped back-to-back
by gender, the kitchen like the tap-
room of an old-style pub, each half

a mystery to the other, though admittedly not one
of especial importance —
told me & Gav about the time at Linden —
Linden Hall, that is, a country mansion,
back in the day a private residence
though subject of late to swift changes of ownership

as chain after chain swoops in & gives up
on its modest links & restaurant
flogging unseasonable salmon —
flavourless, hence the smoke —
at Linden when, in loopy old age, Eve Adamson,
her God-given name, decides to summon —

'Oz', I nearly said, but no,
she wouldn't've used the diminutive
for it wouldn't've been right
to abbreviate
such a fine old Northumbrian name;
and besides, 'Oswald' was his *middle* name,

so if she *were* to drop
the formalities — & she *wasn't* — then her Ladyship
would have called him 'William'
for he'd been born
back when my people, should I have one, tended
to take the name of a king or a saint —

summon him with a tinkling of her bedside bell
and 'Young?' she shrills
and there he stands,
her servant-to-be-commanded,
and this time what she's after's that brace of snipe
lately shot on her estate,

so Oz has to take off, find them in the woodshed
where they've been hung two days,
pluck them — 'like shuffling
a greasy deck of cards' — and he'd have been
whistling all this while,
for he'd ever have a tune in his head

till Tina put a stop to it — 'Ozzie: *whisht!*' —
on the grounds that it interfered
with one or other hearing aid,
which, fair's fair, were cranked so high
they'd give a yelp of feedback if you got too close,
like when you turned the other cheek

for her to plant a goodbye kiss —
Oz: 'There's Jimi Hendrix tuning up' —
and cook them in the traditional style,
which, I'll tell you so you know, calls for you
to skewer the poor things on their own beaks —
then it's in the cooker, then it's on the plate,

then it's quick as that she's ate
them, brains & all, while William Oswald Young
holds his hat & holds his tongue
looking at nowt but a brace of beaks
laid crosswise in her lap,
one of which she now takes up & uses for a toothpick.

TO A HALVER

And the little screaming fact that sounds through all history...
John Steinbeck

O halver, O haffa, O half-brick: your battened-down
century of faithful service in a pit village terrace
forgotten now you've broken loose; now you're at large
on CCTV, flackering out of kilter till you bounce
like far-flung hail rebounding off the riot squad —
or kissing the away support a fond goodbye —
or anyhow let fly, as fifty years ago
someone aimed you at my father's skull
while he was being shepherded down Rutherglen Road
when it was raining bottles, when it was raining hammers & nails
after an Old Firm fixture — the decider: I exist
because you missed and broke his collarbone —
I weigh you now against the good you've done.
St George's Hill, when Cromwell's cavalry advance
we find you, or your country cousins, apt & good,
versatile in the hands of the True Levellers;
now Banksy has a laugh replacing you with flowers;
and what about your bit-part in that dockyard stand-off?
The gates swing-to, the scabs clock on —
as to the nitty-gritty of whose side you're on,
you stay, as they say, ahead of the curve.
But you were there at Peterloo & you were there
at Brixton. You were all the rage in Meadow Well.
Your ancestors were with us in the cave
before the wheel before the fire & ever since
we've never been without you: all our high designs
can be reduced to you. You stand for stunted hope
grown wild among the backyard odds & sods
where the snubbed toaster and the jilted BMX

jockey for position with the unacknowledged honesty.
O root & seed of boxed-in lives! O token of dissent!
How often have I seen you in the thick of it
and raised my arm against you? On pitted tarmac,
by the gutted community centres of besieged estates —
borne as a gift or hurled down like a prophecy —
I've seen you taken up & even in the playground,
hidden in a snowball, you followed hard upon.
You've come a long way from the clay-pit, worked out & abandoned;
a long way from the vanished kilns of Langley & Eldon —
here: let me launch you on another posthumous career,
earthbound comet, stub of destiny, throwback. I have a
soft spot for you, so go on: make something happen,
O clod, O totem of the unaccommodated, O halver —
history's ellipsis point, sign to which we must attend —
when words fail may you always be at hand.

LABOURERS, ALLENDALE, C.1875
after Edward Thomas

Three cloistered cells, three dim rooms once
part of a biggin left long since
to starlings, rats & ruin. What remains is held
together by sun-bleached prints —
horsewomen, the gentry's dogs, well-bred
children — an abacus, a generations-old
christening spoon, memorial cards of the dead
who left for Spain, for good, the last hill levelled.

The squat, wrought-iron pick that opened
untold veins of lead nor ever jarred
the fingers that wore the handle smooth stands guard
over the kitchen now, an ornament
kept like the obsolete *fornenst* & *glim*
he still uses should anyone, most of all him,
need minding on that, till the blackleg year
of £9 a ton, he was a miner here.

His wife remembers — she who was so tall
she'd had to stoop for the chapel door, who now
bent like a thorn in the law's west wind
can't see September apples till they fall;
can't, as she walks an upland mile
daily to fetch spring water for the cow,
carry the pail without it sweeps the ground:
in such small freedoms the royal roads end.

He cuts wood, makes hay — no one thatches
better, his haystacks pinnacled like churches;
in spring traps moles to pin on briars,
works twigs into cocoons that hold till fur
and bone are blown to dust. Now on a whim
he stops to down tools, puff a tab & think,
expecting to be paid for thinking. Death
or the workhouse twelve month shy of him.

She can watch for hours a black grouse peck at ants
in the dock roots, ruddocks bounce
careless & close... Tonight he has a drink
on him, says he reckons he has heard
in The Golden Lion the gossip of the universe:
swindles, murders, horse races, these foreign wars,
the wastefulness of the poor... The printed word
inspires his trust, his telling of it hers.

UNDERSONG

i.m. Bill Griffiths

I am storing fifty-one seeds of Goatsbeard:
so I can sow again.
Now I have lost them. Now I search again.
Bill Griffiths

Here's something for the children who worked down the mine:
the trappers on the tram-ways & the barrow-ways;
the bairns who, for their pains,
were made shovers & skeekers, hewers & headsmen,
landing-lads & foal-putters;

the ones who, when their lives
could not be carried in the common tongue,
invented speech to fit: North's undersong,
a dialect within a dialect, the kind of thing
(you'd have said) poets like to take the credit for.

And, quoted in Parliamentary Papers, 1842,
Volume 16: Commissioners' Reports
on working practice down the mine,
here's something from a boy — an unnamed Seaham boy —
who went down at the age of eight:

I had six candles from my father.
I liked it very well at first
but then I had an accident.
The tub broke my arm in two places.
I had a coal fall on my forehead
and the mark remains, and will always remain.
I got no smart money.

THE BUTTONED LIP

Surely thou also art one of them; for thy speech bewrayeth thee.
Matthew, 26:73

Wise child, with an ear for the condescending tone, an eye
for patronage, how did you come so far with it intact:
the last — no: latest — vestige of native dialect to betray
itself when you were drunk, unbuttoned in mixed company,
leaving you to stand, for all your la-de-dah, corrected?
O patron saint of little piggies what should've stayed at yem,
how does it feel to hear your words fly up, die of shame,
and then resume their station in the afterlife; to lie
awake in the wee, wee hours convening your symposium
(here a double-barrelled Communist, there a Tory derelict
mouthing off on regional-identity-as-fictive-construct:
perhaps we may conclude the poet's prime responsibility
must be to language rather than to place...), only this time
for the record raise your hand & open your mouth to speak?

THE PROPHET
after Pushkin

Once
in the desert
a six winged seraph
hailed me at the crossroads.
He just reached out with his fingertips:
like that
my eyes were stunned
with the vision of a hawk
reeling on its first flight from the nest;
like that
my ears filled
with thundering timpani
the threshing of angels' wings
the stir of blue whales rolling in the deep
and the groan of vines that stretched across the earth.
And he tore
my blabbing tongue
out by the root, his hand
engrossed with blood — and between
my lips squeezed a wise serpent's venom.
Next he splits
my ribcage; now
lifts the cowering heart
from its cradle — casting it away
to plant almost tenderly in its place a spitting coal...
Friend, I was laid out like a corpse when the voice came to me:
Prophet: stand.
See. Hear. Your fate
is to wander by sea and land.
To be my will. To find my people out
and to brand their hearts with the Word.

I.M. TERRY KELLY

Fallen Angels —
I was almost sorry
you'd never hear
it, but no,

surely you, yes,
you'll've caught it
yonks ago
before it dropped

just as, should these
lines I'm in
the process of writing
for you, Terry,

ever appear
(as they do here)
then true to form
you'd've had to let me know

you saw them
coming like a slow
train all the way from
Jarrow to Juarez

Newcastle to New
Jerusalem
or wherever it is
you've got to

COMEUPPANCE

I liked the way she said it,
like getting a fleck
of baccy off her lip:
You'll get your comeuppance.
It had a smack — more
than a smack — of inheritance,
the way she'd spit
those plosives out —
think *spite*, think *pittance*,
think *precious little* —
as I ducked outside
to pick a dandelion:
You'll get your comeuppance.
I took her word for it.

Her fear of dandelions!
We'd plant them in her slippers
or the cutlery drawer — ridiculous,
the way the littlest thing
betokened something —
her toothache, her bunions,
her illiterate faith in language —
the way an idle word,
a bitten-off breath,
could seed the day with auguries;
the way if you said *pig*
she wouldn't leave the house
but sit, fixed in her chair,
the way she sits today,

cast up on widowhood
like something brittle
while her daughters fuss about her.
Tight-lipped, she'll never speak
about their father. She'll die
asking if it's fair,
her fine-spun puff of hair —
flustered, pitiful,
backlit by the nightlight,
in the end
neither here nor there —
like a blown clock, or
yes, *Pittle-the-bed*,
as she might have said.

A LYKE-WAKE DIRGE

A queen in hiding —
bespoke in whispers,
exiled among her defenders —
she took her last illness
at a stately pace,
settee to settee,
culminating in
a triumphant run
of deathbed scenes
that ended
the only way it could
in the gloomy menagerie
of her own front room.
Being her favourite

I was called upon
to pass a night there
the week she died.
Sole witness to the cold
association of
antimacassars and the slow
gleam of the clock's
pendulum, I saw a brass
poker, tongs & brush
pass for ornaments;
I saw *Scotland the Brave* —
a framed print of highland cattle
camped in a hazy blush
of heather & Scotch mist...

I slept like a cat —
and still she woke me
pressing a ransom
into my hands…
Hers was the first love
I knew I could not return.
I write these lines
in memory of
a sun-bleached spoil
of *People's Friend*s —
she placed, once, in the Love Darg —
and the new gas fire
where a Davy lamp stood guard
over a mouse made of coal.

THE MATTER

as if heaven cared
John Wieners

After sleepy time, pain, After sin, self-knowledge.
Let the world be all we waken to. Let mother
lick a hanky, kneel to rub the matter
from our clogged eyes: there. After an age

of small mercies, the predictable travesty.
After a lifetime of supportable losses,
a woman bibbed in gin & vomit rises
to disavow a prodigal & would-be

righteous anger. Let dormative virtue take
effect. Let one he knows, but not to speak to,
smile recognisably. Non è fuggito.
Now be a love for heaven's sake

and let it go. Who wants to make a scene?
Her least of all, who would & will affect
to misconceive me at my most direct;
knew I meant well, never knows what I mean.

SOBER-HEARTED MAN BLUES

Woke up this morning
Lord I couldn't get drunk
Up with the larks
Mixing whisky & wine
Fooling no one
Slurring my words
Fell over in the street
No really I'm fine

Me O me I'm a sober-hearted man
I'll remember this tomorrow
It's time I dug up my drunken woman
& put her in a wheelbarrow

Told my baby
Lord I loved her so very much
Very, very much
Very much indeed
O what could I do
I know what I said
I know what I'm saying
O what can you do

When you're a sober-hearted man
I'll remember this tomorrow
It's time I dug up my drunken woman
& put her in a wheelbarrow

Told my bosom friends
Lord give me some warning
No you can't just drop in

Any old time
Don't want you to have to hear me
Talking sense
Don't want you to see me
In my prime

'cause I'm a sober-hearted man
I'll remember this tomorrow
It's time I dug up my drunken woman
& put her in a wheelbarrow

O mother dear mother
If I don't get drunk soon
I believe it's all over
For your blue-eyed boy
I've been stone cold
Since I got off the train
What works for you
Won't work for me

Poor me, poor me,
Pour me another
You'll remember that tomorrow
It's time I dug up my drunken woman
& put her in a wheelbarrow

THE SEVEN JOYS OF FAILURE

The first joy of failure
is relief at the success avoided:
more properly, the consequences of success;
and the prospect of a quietude,
absence of ambition
passing for humility.

The second joy
is pecuniary, for when vision is reduced
to the things of the world
it will most often find itself accompanied
by the sorts of behaviours
that go with, lead to, or derive from, money.

The third joy
is private and hardly to be spoken of;
but joy nonetheless, however gruesome,
at having our self-loathing proven true,
the certainty so many tender doubts defended
rudely confirmed.

The fourth joy
is public: at the warmth of fellow-feeling,
the heartiness of the embrace,
smiling enquiries as to our future plans
if any, unstinting camaraderie,
the glad-hand welcome of the world.

The fifth joy
is the sweetest joy: the care of the clear-eyed
who supported us without belief,
and built a store for the inevitable day
we thought would never come:
day of their triumph.

The sixth joy
is dangerous: the temptation to believe
that something may yet come of this;
that we have fallen into wakefulness
merely to enact the dream;
that the final crash was but a station.

The seventh joy
is satisfaction: claiming the comfortable chair
from which we see life in a true perspective,
and things as we suppose they are
align with every circumstance,
never to rise, never to want again.

THE TAWNY OWL

There was this owl — I used to see him
perched on his branch in the not-yet-dusk,
poised like a diver taking his time.
I'd look out from my attic room;
I'd look up from the dishes — there he'd be,
weighing his options… then suddenly
let fall himself in a low glide the length of the terraced garden,
bob over the churchyard wall, and be gone.

His flight was silent, silencing.
His disappearance had the force of apprehension.
Never saw a kill. Never saw
a mouse limp in his beak, though I remember it.
Was not, as I once thought I'd be,
brushed by his wing.

Unable to escape, I learned to see.
The price of clarity.
I remember Dad teaching me how to tell
a two-stroke engine by its sound & smell
and me wishing I cared.
I remember a powder-blue hymnal
waiting on each chair in the assembly hall.
I remember mouthing the words *God* & *Lord*
to see what would happen. I remember
seeing what happened.
I remember Foxe's *Book of Martyrs*
and I remember Findus Crispy Pancakes.
I remember when my grudge
was flavour of the month,
sipping elderberry pop
like it was crème-de-menthe
from a plastic champagne flute,
my prize-winning smile
for the sniggering judge
(*Listen to your accent!*)
and all the names she could drop.
I remember applause
is the beginning of abuse, abuse
the beginning of applause.
I remember my accuser's gassy lies,
that wretched voice:
tutored, plausible, smart-casual — like his verse.
I remember the diary I should not have read,
last summer's dress
bagged up for charity.
I remember Gus, dead

at sixteen — a dodgy batch
of methylenedioxymethamphetamine
or, as he'd've had it, a bad dab
of rhubarb & custard —
and no nationwide campaign
to raise awareness. And
for yet a very little while
I will remember Mam sniffing her knees in the bath
and me asking why & her saying
because they smell of salt and it's nice.
At that time the priest Eli was ruling in Judea
and the Ark of the Covenant
was captured by the Philistines.

So what. He told a lie. So what.
It explained a thing or two about a thing or two.
It wasn't anything that somebody else would never do.
A little one. So what.

     There's a well —

He put it at the heart of things.
It just seemed to go right to the heart of things.
It seemed right, or just, to sing from the heart, or something.

     There's a well in this world —

He told a lie. He wore it like a mask.
He worked at it and later it worked him.
A little one. The first. Don't ask.
It worked. Of course it worked. Don't ask, don't ask.

       There's a well in this world — should you drink from it,
       your thirst will be worse than a curse. There's a well —
       O but it's better not to think of it!
       You'll have to tell your friends —
       they'll thank you for it!

He drank. If you can call it a well.

A FORM OF WORDS

Just as, after the affair, when I knew I was in the clear
but came down with trismus of all things
and had, needs must, to post the "finest sashimi in Brooklyn"
through the half-inch letterbox
between my upper & my lower incisors
    poking it in there with the chopsticks
yearning to contribute in a non-confrontational way
to Miss X & her sister & her sister's Awful Husband's *conversazione*
on blue fin versus yellow fin
and then the "whole environmental thing"
(this from a cunt who ate a turtle in Indonesia)
I was saying nothing —
I'm saying nothing now.

    And if I had to do it all again
    I wouldn't.
    John Berryman said that: I'm not saying it.

And just as, when those two blokes came to replace the boiler,
and asked would I like to pay cash
and I said "Nee probs" —
    and watched them carry gear in from the obligatory once-white van
    and watched them work, and saw how, though both young,
    the elder laboured to the younger,
    but as they worked in brotherly quiet
    an hour passed before I realised
    the older lad was "touched"
    as I was taught to say, and how I liked the way
    the younger never lorded it, how
    even when the elder put the radiator back
    before the skirting board, or tripped

over the blowtorch he'd left lying,
no remonstrations followed,
a ticking-off over bait in the van perhaps, but still
a hundred unregarded acts of kindness
daily & of a gentleness conspicuously absent
in certain other unacknowledged legislators —
I can't say I object to what is being proposed.

And that we must learn to leave the table
when love is no longer being served —
Charles Aznavour said that: I'm not saying it.

And while I'm not saying a form of words couldn't be found
I still think of them two blokes e.g. in Boards of Study
at the Russell Group institution where I am currently on probation
as I bask in the glare of my colleague's world-alienating pedantry
yes I sit like Caesar in his tent
where the maps are spread
and I think of them two blokes
and it's like a hole in my head
and I think of them two blokes
or else I meditate on what it means
to take your first full-time job at the age of 37
or on the nature of failure generally.

When you arrive at the very bottom
you will hear knocking from below.
Thanks, Stanisław Jerzy Lec.

And just as, when I am getting through the drinks
that follow the interminable Board of Study
at the Russell Group institution where I am currently on probation
and the ego-chutney's coming down like hail —
    "...what I would say to inner-city blacks is:

     hip-hop is the problem, not the solution…"
  "…I saw your *TLS* piece on Basil Bunting and I have to say:
          fourteen isn't twelve…"
  "…of course the thing you mustn't say is:
          Islam is truly evil…" —
I might see if a form of words can't be found
for the time in Brooklyn
when Miss X accidentally locked us out of the apartment we'd been
     renting
that last morning while the taxi purred & we panicked
     and there was 15 feet of pure white snow & it was 6 a.m.
     and the landlord wasn't answering & the gods were asleep
     and we were like so do we call the cops or something
     and eventually I just kicked the door in
          and really it gave so easily
          I can't say I shouldn't have done it sooner
     and we grabbed our cases & caught the taxi after all
          which meant we'd make the flight
and, portered through wintry pre-dawn streets,
hearing Jay Z & Alicia Keys on the radio at that very moment sing
what had hitherto seemed a gormless knees-up of a song
about Manhattan's ability to confer
a non-specific sense of optimism on the visitor,
I felt imbued with possibly dubious agency —
I now suspect my silences contain the best of me.

     And I'm a man who likes talking
     to a man who likes to talk.
     I never said that, Sidney Greenstreet said it.

And even now a form of words can surely be found
for my feelings when, packing up to move on
from one shitty rental to another, shittier rental

as I have done on an annual basis since the age of 18
I found the watch I'd lost the day we moved in
behind a box of books
where it had lain 6 months pressed to the damp wall
so the leather strap had furred into a caterpillar
with spiny hairs of mould
and when I fished it up by its buckle
I could hear the timepiece ticking on oblivious.

    Omissions are not accidents.
    Marianne Moore. You knew that one.

And surely at this stage in the game, surely we can speak
of Shorty, booted out first thing, early bird
breakfasting on a fun-size Mars bar
or trailing home through puddles, dry eyed,
indifferent as the weather... Surely it's time to share
our knowing he'd been "interfered with"
if not by his mam (a "single mother...
you can smell it on her breath...")
then by one or other
of her men — we'd see them at the gates, all the cars
Shorty got a go in!
               We said nowt at the time, the foremost
lesson of that fucking circus
driven home when Miss Bird (newly in post,
soon to fly south) asked what we'd like to be when we grew up —
on his turn Shorty sniggered "A rapist"
and everyone cracked up.
He'd "got life" (been expelled) before the bell went. Class.

    Drank so much gin & whisky
    sweet mama I can hardly talk.
    That's not me that's Blind Willie McTell.

And might it now be possible to try your patience further
I said may I be permitted, reader, majesty, to tax your patience further
and find a form of words for how it felt to see —
    after the bailiffs had fucked off
    with a truck load of furniture, indoor slides for the bairns,
    the Xbox, microwave, deep fat fryer,
    IKEA light fittings fancied-up with glitter glue,
    widescreen plasma telly on tick,
    the sandwich toaster he must've won at the Hoppings
    and even, get this, her *cross trainer*;
    after they'd been turfed out too,
    him not all there ("touched"), her pregnant, a month to Christmas —
my neighbours-across-the-way's landlord stopping by for a poke about
        (he even brought a flask of tea
        so he could make an afternoon of it)?
And can I hope to improve on the form of words
he later found for his compleynt
that having acquired so much tat
he'd have to rent the place as furnished next time round
which was frankly a pain in the balls
or else offload the junk somehow or other
though he'd get nothing for it
because "nothing was worth anything these days"?

Your silence will not protect you:
Audre Lorde, I only appropriate what you were saying.

And surely one day soonish
there will be season due
to speak of Old Ray next door
who'd stop by now & then for a bit moan
about the number of "Pakis" on the bus, or the number of tracksuits
queuing for heroin in Boots, or the milk from the Co-op
being radioactive & Polish,

or just to count the bottles in my recycling bin: Old Ray
to whom I spoke as little as possible
disliking utterly & without reserve his manner, opinions, face & smell —
and then after the stroke, his maimed voice
seeping through the wall
as he chewed the ear off his daughter-in-law
    who must've jealoused Old Ray
    had monies squirrelled away
a bass mope like farting in the bath
as though no form of words could be found.

O pray for me St Sasha
in fluent русский or via
yr unusually expressive eyebrows
when you remove the bone as one might draw
a hairpin, smear the rollmop on black bread
and indulge my little
pretence that the Russian deli at Elephant & Castle is
St Petersburg.

O pray for me St Edwin
with all the fervency the envious angels will allow
when, picked out on the dripping verges,
I feel against my cheek
the blowsy petals of the rhododendron.

O pray for me St Effy:
walk with me under the viaduct to Flass Vale
where goldfinches chivvy up &
    off across the way;
teach me to live the hours not the years
and do, please, to my dizzy, boring, Venlafaxine thinking what
Oz's whistling once did to Sunday afternoons.

O pray for me St Jeff
from the snowball fight with Kiyonaga
to the mountains of Hiroshige
I am with you on the bridge in spirit
under the foxes' bridal procession
and when you say so we'll "stare down, see only
the sun at the ripples, the glint
of light a sugared glaze…"
for without you I am Cobra Verde
and I never had a friend in my life.

O patron of the honest overlooked, St Bob,
gentle man with border reiver blood in yr veins
when you are beach-combing Boaty's Bay
for sea glass washed up from the abandoned works —
mermaids' tears, fish eyes from punty rods,
frosted pearls & end-of-day glass —
pray for me now
I am becoming part of the immense
indifference of the world.

This state-of-the-nation bulletin for J.P.N.

LAST POEM

i.m. Derek Mahon

We value them, the voices
that need us least, who speak
with honest subtlety
to ironies beyond us,
who slip our grasp and go
whistling down endless
celestial colonnades
of — no, not astral planes
where the dream-soul wanders,
but airport corridors,
bus stations, the Gare du Nord,
a beach house in Goa,
testing posterity
with promises to break.

Who wouldn't picture you
somewhere refurbishing
your echo-chamber stanzas,
making Parnassus ring
with the clattering of a battered
Olympia, tricks of tone
and scrambled rhyme-schemes drawing
dry-eyed epiphanies
from Dionysian mysteries,
if you didn't guard against
such hopes with the *nonchalance
of complete despair*,
as against the sublime you almost
perfectly renounced...

All fade oblivionwards...
That I can believe; still, when
our attitudes at last
become us, and we threaten
to stiffen into posture,
if nothing else your words
may release us into gesture —
or so I tell myself
as I scribble these rough numbers
and lay my little wreath:
I got to meet you, once,
and gave my name for silence
and 'best wishes, Derek Mahon'.
My *Life on Earth* remembers.

II

THE ACTS OF OBLIVION

In Meadowes, where our sports were wont to be
(And, where we playing wantonly have laine)
Men sprawling in their blood, we now doe see;
Grim postures, of the dying, and the slaine
— George Wither, 'Campo-Musae', 1643

There is no remembrance of former things; neither shall there be
any remembrance of things that are to come with those that shall
come after.
— Ecclesiastes, 1:11

TO HISTORY

To you the rind, to you the bitter fruit.
A pointer bitch fawns on your right royal sleeve
while you stare down a plea for clemency.
The towers fall. Magnolia blooms. You see
the Emperor Valerian flayed alive.
Who draws you out draws out a mandrake root.

THE PARASITE

5 May 1640

Algernon Percy, 10th Earl of Northumberland,
naked as innocence before the mirror,
ties his necklace — fine blue silk, adorned
with an enamel-gold medallion of St George
lancing the dragon: very good! — and then
in a dramatic gesture only I observe
sweeps his riding cloak about his shoulders.
The left side bears a star-shaped aureole
emblazoned in silver thread. There. Admirably done.

One hour from now the Privy council will request
that he, newly appointed Lord Protector, raise
an army against the rebel Scots. My host —
Commander-in-Chief and the King's favourite, yes,
but also scrutinant of his coffers and flat broke —
gives me a run-through of his stalling tactics:
To raise tax on your majesty's prerogative
will only meet a fraction of the cost
and fail as surely as the last war did — no, no!

It's time. We are accompanied to Whitehall
by footmen, coachmen, and postilions
all liveried in blue silk with silver wire,
the Garter round a crescent: his heraldic badge;
to think — the pity of it! — he must risk all this
persuading His Majesty to compromise…
Steel-rimmed carriage wheels rattle, pebbles scatter,
London turns in its bed to face the wall
and my host tries once more to hammer it out:

Majesty, might it be politic to affect
a superstition on the need for parliament's
moral — that is, financial — backing when at war?
That sounds more like it. Alighting on Queen's Road
he takes the steps two at a time
allowing the slightest of smiles to play
about his lips. A hopeful gleam of first light
flashes back at him from the paving stones
and he feels a passing dizziness come over him…

Inside, my host is busy with confections,
a crucible in which I'm gently crushed,
part of the soup, part of the recipe
that makes up Algernon's compendium.
Since the blood meal when we met six days ago
I've shadowed him close as an apprentice.
Right now I'm gazing through the jelly of his eyes
as through stained glass. I see a cat-faced man,
a half-smile glutted with contempt: the king.

Suddenly I will declare myself with seizures,
enlargement of the liver and the spleen,
convulsions and religious mania,
keeping my host from the field and the court.
And should historians of the future ask
If Percy had prevailed, might civil war
have been prevented? — I will answer that
my kind, preferring time to history,
seriously incline towards a longer view.

THE ROGUE

Being Two Letters from Col. Henry Marten, believed to have been written while he was imprisoned on the Holy Island of Lindisfarne, the first being written to his Brother, George, and the second being a Familiar Letter to his Lady of Delight.

I

In the minutes of committees
    to see off Laud & Strafford;
in the hour of choice —
    absolute tyranny
or, whisper it, no king? —
    to draft the Protestation;
in the day of reckoning
    to take from the Royal mews
horses apt otherwise
    to be employed against us;
and then in '42,
    the Stuart mustering troops,
to stand before my tenants
    tearing the royal commission:
somebody had to do it!
    (*Stultorn incurate vigor*
malus ulcera vexat —
    George, it was my imprudence
saved me from the axe:
    what return have you on yours?)
And they called this 'agitation'.
    They remarked on my 'asperity'.
And I: *Is it unlawful*
    1,000 men should meet
and beat a drum? Is not

kingship forfeitable?
And Pym, Lord Stepaside,
    he wanted my head for that —
might have had it too,
    but finding half the House
in debt to me, me likewise
    to the other half's creditors,
since I, not avoiding
    injury to my fortune,
had implicated all
    my mortgages & bonds
so thoroughly with those
    of my right honourable friends
that to tease out one string
    wd surely unclew all,
settled instead upon
    a two-week stint in gaol
then — exile to Sleepyshire.
    3 years I have to pass
as *Marten, Gentleman Farmer,*
    Hinton Waldrist, Berkshire;
3 years of village gossip
    with Sexby, Allen, Lockyer,
before — and this would be
    January, '46,
so just about the time
    France ran low on virgins
and you sailed for Barbados —
    O sweet Act of Oblivion!
May all my sins be thus
    discovered/disremembered!

    Speaking of oblivion, much thanks
    for the shipment of dark rum:

it does my heart good
to know what 200 acres of sugar yields
with 6 years cultivation
under the Caribbean sun
in the hands of so industrious a man as yrself.
Thanks, too, for the tobacco:
the last & quite the worst I ever smoked.
But really, what with wine from the Canaries
and this half-sweet Herefordshire cider from my tenants,
I cannot think my annual vintner's bill is justified:

    22 barrels of 6th beer
    3 kinderkins of 16th ale
    1 barrel of strong beer
                    £9 7s. 2d.   ???

(Last month we dined on goose,
roast beef, dressed veal, pork, tongue,
tripe, mutton, capon, lamb,
mince pies & cheese —
they say Pym ran a book
on which would catch me first:
my creditors or gout —
please disregard the stories
of my continuing incarceration as
so many paper bullets!)

Any road, I was back —
    brass balls, George, & sharp elbows —
meantime everything
    has gone to hell of course
with the Stuart on the run
    until the Scots have got him
garrisoned in Newcastle

and only Chaloner will speak
against the auld betrayal —
    Pym slaughtering Irishmen
just to keep Ollie quiet,
    both of 'em descended
from our gallant ancestors
    buried in Palestine,
whither they were carried
    desirous to recover
yᵉ Holy Land, and beat
    yᵉ whole world in to righteous
Christianity —
    really, had not his Nibs
signed on with the Covenanters,
    i.e. plainly writ his faults
upon his own forehead,
    I don't know there was much
anyone could have done…
    And Ollie more than happy
taking credit for the rout,
    the massacre at Preston —
scant mention of yours truly
    and that *Bastard kind of Militia
called the County Troop* —
    then the great purge Lilburne
warned us all against
    when we cast out the moderates —
the nodders, the noddees —
    *ignavum fucos pecus
a praesepibus arcent!* —
    the heavy lifting done
by detachments from the regiments of Col. Pride —
    'Tom Pride': most satisfactory! —
until, sure we had won

the people's sovereignty,
we delivered parliament
    to Ireton & his grandees.
And Ollie more than happy.

Being a man of business
you will have scant use for poesy
(nor can I blame you there),
still you may be amused
to read this specimen:

> *Here comes SIR HENRY MARTYN*
> *As good as ever pist,*
> *This wenching beast*
> *Has whores at least*
> *A thousand on his list:*
> *This makes the Devil laugh,*
> *So good a friend to see…*

I wd thank the (unsigned) author of *The Bloody Bed-roll*
for his bestowal of a knighthood, but assure him
that though I reckon I have now met with 2 devils
I never yet heard either of them laugh.

And then I'm named commissioner
    to the High Court of Justice,
and Davenant, you know
    Sir William Davenant,
he comes a-begging help
    for they want to string him up,
and really I can't say
    he doesn't have it coming,
but he's spilling at the sides
    with stories of our father —

O the youthful japes
    they once shared blah blah blah —
so for old sake's sake
    I stand before the House
proclaiming him *An old*
    and rotten rascal too
impure for sacrifice —
    and thus I save his neck
not that he thanks me for it,
    and in the end we do it
we get the Stuart tried
    and on the scaffold, no one
pressing for it harder
    than the man himself.
But let me set down this:
    had I divined that the Axe
wch lopped the late King's head
    wd prove so apt a stirrup
for our first false General,
    I'd sooner have consented
to my own death than his.

    Now: about my new cloak.
    Fur trim, jet pin, lace-lined,
    buttoning at the neck…
    and my suit faced with taffeta,
    and my hose lined with calico…
    £17 8s. 5d.
    Had to get my portrait done
    to justify the cost.
    For it well becomes a man
    to honour and respect
    and seize on all that life
    reveals; and if he finds

his table spread in strange places,
even in the presence
of cordial enemies,
should he give over the feast?
I think not! And my bow
has a string or three yet,
and one of 'em will take
supposing luck should serve —
till then I shall remain
yr very loving brother,
proprietor & bankrupt,
adulterer, philanthropist,
broad-faced sott & gambler,
ugly rascal, spymaster,
Right Honourable Member,
whoremonger & regicide —
     Honest Harry Marten.

II

My last & only love,
though I were sure to live
an hundred years, & thou
not half so many hours,
'tis a filthy long while since
we either saw or heard
from one another, no?
Yet don't let's chide, dear love.
Our friendly porter says
we may soon meet again —
before the month is out,
he promises — and next time
we shall not want for Rhenish

wine to tipple thy nose in…
How are my little bantlings?
Is Peggy still our singer?
Have Bacon-hog and Poppet
been back to Mr Hall's gardens
to tickle his gooseberry-bushes?
I reckon they will take
every word they hear
to be an errant lie
when they are come of age:
the world is grown so false!
Loder stopped by to pay
a kind of visit, bestowing
great quantities of words
and not a rag of money,
but his news, such as it was,
is not worth gaping after:
all my estates shall be
devoured by the Duke of York
(some day perhaps his grandson
will disentangle the jointures,
statutes & mortgages
I left them cumbered with)
and soon a tribe of bailiffs,
catch-poles & the like
will be exasperated
against thee, and will have thee
by hook or by crook —
why, is it not a comfort
to know what we must trust to?
The skill, I suppose, lies not
in being weather-wise
but weather-proof: we two
must throw off all we can

and snug like humble snails
within our very selves,
that is, our minds, which no one
but we can touch... Well, well —
I am, I think, a piece of a philosopher!
But thou & I have leaned
on many a broken reed
ere now, and afterwards
lit on a sounder staff,
so my poor soul puts on
a bushel of patience — thus:
perhaps the bill won't pass;
perhaps the Lords won't pass it;
perhaps the King gives way
to his friends in setting this on
so he may have the honour
of pardoning to himself;
perhaps some names may be
excepted in one House
or in the other; perhaps
thy Dear may be one of them...
Will any butter stick
upon my bread? I say:
He that hath time, hath life.
Now, I gave the bearer monies
to buy a neck of mutton,
two pound of candles, one of rush,
a sixpenny loaf, some beer,
and sparaguss, and coals,
and left for you a token
in the belly of my letter.
(I hope to send thee soon
a bottle of rare sack —
but thou must keep it cool

in water with salt-peter.)
Meantime look upon my brats:
is not thy Dear among them?
For has not one of 'em
his face? Or has not one
his brains or else his mirth?
Look most upon that last,
for it is just the best
thing in the world — a thing
never yet taken from me...
According to Lucian,
having reached the banks
of Acheron our soul
will be stripped of character:
all we would freely own —
humility, patience, wit —
and all we would overlook:
pride's delicacy would slow us;
our ponderous hypocrisy
unbalance Charon's skiff;
pity, real or feigned,
would implicate us in
the suffering of others
and blind us to our own;
so it is the fop must lose
his vanity, the athlete
all his prized perfections —
at least, so Lucian says,
and very like, for here
in this life as you see
we must divest ourselves
of all that we possess —
first all that we can spare,
and then all that remains:

we exercise our will
in ordering our losses —
very like & proper
to afterwards be stripped
of the passions that possess us...
Well, well I will spend no more
ink upon thee now,
but bottle up my business
for thy ugly ears. Therefore
good morrow, Monkey-face.

    Thine own
        H. Marten.

LORD HEARSAY'S PALACE
after Ovid, Metamorphoses, *XII, 39-63*

Once divided, truth divides forever.
Marius Kociejowski

A world much like our own, mistempered & twi-natured,
    three-fold purgatorial zone
where Lord Hearsay sits with all his might upon the tallest,
    narrowest chair, the barstool throne
from which he helps both living & dead to die in that open
    fortress where no locks hold,
whose hallways buzz with bullshitters, each pushing their
    self-branded narrative, their spin
emptying out in the whorl of an ear; where fake news stays
    news, broadcast & gone but soon
repeating back, re-echoing with iterations, no dead air
    allowed, all filled
with hard-to-place murmurings, captious chit chat melting
    to a soft, insinuating drone
like far-off tidal breakers or the first tremor of thunder
    Jupiter calls down;
where, were you able to take the measure of a fiction, it
    would elaborate and groan
with new addition, tittle tattle, evil report; where everyone's
    briefed & puffed & trolled
by imitators; where carefree Gossip flat-shares with
    Credulity; where you'll be hailed
by Anxiety who'll say anything once and simple Truth who
    doesn't want to be consoled:
there, slum landlord, overseer of whatever comes to pass,
    from these waters of Tyne
to Acheron, in Heaven or on Earth, Lord Hearsay watches
    over all the world.

SAPPHICS FOR ELIZABETH LILBURNE
1649

Where is he whose patience can suffer one more
sainted devil ministering independence?
Don't you think our interest equal? Tell us,
    did you imagine

we would be so sottish or stupid as to
bide, cook, sew, mend, seeing our peace & welfare
broken down, trod underfoot by one who rocks
    nations as cradles,

hooks & lands Leviathan but to swiftly
bridle it, demands that the blackbird freely
sing the tribute owed to a fenced-in meadow
    once held in common?

We were not your trees by the river, quaking
aspen, sere-leafed, fated to fall in season:
righteous anger bested us. Earthly power
    rules absolutely.

Lone, aloof, all friends in the tower, unbraided
cords to implicate in good time, mute burdens
set to music by the succeeding children
    England so prizes —

trusted stranger, hear what your broken language
makes of us, our worldly accomplishment of
martyred pride, our faith in the promised day when
    history fails us.

WELL DONE, THOU GOOD AND FAITHFUL SERVANT
1662

This is the ballad of a faithful servant
  As loyal as he was true:
His name it was George Downing and
  That's 'Sir George' to you...

O the king sat on the Privy Council
  Drinking the wine-red blood
And promising to forgive & forget
  As all good Christians should.

But once he got behind closed doors
  The king soon changed his fettle:
'I'm not in the forgiving vein —
  I've got Dad's score to settle!

O where will I find a true-hearted man
  To track his regicides down
And trick 'em to trust us & face our good justice,
  Those traitors to the crown?

For as I suppose everyone knows
  They're in old Amsterdam,
And I look a right stately Johnny-come-lately
  The longer they're on the lam.'

Such was the jolly king's request
  (I mean King Charles II)
So George knelt down, suppressed a frown,
  And just for a moment reckoned...

But our man didn't need to think
    Too hard about this one
Before bringing to mind where he'd most likely find
    Traitors on the run

Because not three years prior to this
    He'd played double with the Dutch
Hunting out spies, though George fought shy
    Of talking about it much

For back in the day Cromwell had in his pay
    No servant so faithful & true
As George Downing, Esquire — back then
    He wasn't 'Sir George' to you —

And he'd won his fame & made his name
    As a good republican would
By rounding up *royalist* sympathisers
    In that same neck of the woods.

So up George stands at the King's command
    And takes his marching orders
To ship 'em home o'er the briny foam
    To be hung, drawn & quartered.

And as it was written so it was done
    And in return the state
Rewarded Downing handsomely
    With some Westminster real estate.

One street in particular
    Bore his name from age to age:
Thus England commemorates
    Its royalist heritage —

If not the man, his works; if not
    The names upon his list,
Then how kindly he served them all —
    I think you get the gist.

SOCIÉTÉ

After Peter Reading

One funny thing about a university education's
the unexpected opportunities it affords you:
in my case, middle-class girls who
(now they tell me) only liked me for my vowels.
One I'd caught on the bounce between a Crispin & a Tristram
took me home to Littlemiddleshire
only to leave me speechless & alone
with a dull-eyed *eau-de-nil* cushion fetishist known as 'Mum'
and port-&-Stilton Daddy who
wouldn't say he was prejudiced, not at all,
just didn't like Asians
or Socialists — and just *did* like traction engines,
battle reenactments, and skiffle music. 'Paul,
when you say English Revolution,
are you referring to the Civil War?
Gosh. And is that what you write *about*?' Still
I put up with it. It must be love.

THE WITCH
after Lucan, Civil War, *Book VI, 507–569*

Black arts, criminal rites, and the heathenish curses of whipped slaves:
such were her cradle songs. Now they offend her: insufferably pious!
New sins, blasphemies yet to be uttered — these make up her study.
Spurning all comfort, she sleeps in the open, or sometimes holes up,
ousting the tenants, in old tombs, waking the dead from their slumber,
pleasing the gods of the underworld. She can convene with the spirits,
eavesdrop, spy out their hidey-holes, learn all their secrets — and not one
god with the stomach to stand in her way! And her face is disfigured,
drawn, lean, sunk-eyed, powdered with quicklime, long hidden from daylight,
weighed down, heavy with handfuls of lank hair. Each time a storm cloud
smothers the stars, then this wretched, untameable animal runs free,
bursts from her charnel house, grasps at the lightning and leaps at the night sky,
chafing the grass with her footprint, blighting the harvest with each step;
even her breath is a poison, inspiring corruption in pure air.
No god ever received from her lips a petition or soft prayer;
never a bull or a bell-sheep offered in sacrifice. Look now:
see her festooning the altars with frankincense stolen from new tombs —
lighting the temple with kindling from funeral pyres is her office.
Yet there is nothing the gods would refuse her. They grant every wish as
soon as it's uttered, no matter how wicked, afraid she'll repeat it.
Sometimes she buries alive men fate has allotted long life —
Death is reluctant, but claim them he must — or reverses the last rites,
quickens a family of corpses, evicting them all from their long home.
Smouldering ashes of children, their thin bones spitting and glowing,
out of the furnace she plucks them, then ransacks the funeral pyre, then
takes as her trophy the torch held tight by the parents in mourning,
scatters the bier so the cerements fly up in billows of black smoke,
scrabbles together the burnt limbs, cinders that reek of decayed meat...
Worse, if the corpse has been laid in a stone tomb, having been drained dry,
all of its jellies and syrups now wasted, congealed to a sour pith,
then she will grow wild, clawing and climbing on top of the body:

frenzied, she scoops out the eyeballs, forces her talon-like fingers
deep in the sockets, and gnaws at the yellowing fingernails that still
grow, for a while, after death. She will chew through the knot in a hanged man's
noose so he drops — warm pulp, like ripe fruit in an orchard — then, yes, she'll
scrape off the crosses, collecting the rain-beaten viscera, sweet meats,
opening the flesh to the mid-day sun so the marrow may soften,
daintily drawing the steel nails out of the crucified man's hands,
squeezing his wounds until blood-clots ooze out, laving the black slime,
using her weight when a tough old sinew resists her enraged bite.
Carrion lying exposed, stripped corpses left after a battle,
these bring her running: the witch appears long before vultures can smell them.
Rather than slice up a carcass, she waits for a wolf pack to close in,
lets them begin — then she snatches the gobbets of meat from their dry mouths.
Nor will she hold back even from murder: whenever a spell needs
warm blood fresh from a pelting aorta, she swiftly procures some.
Next, through a wound in the belly — untimely, unnatural birth! — she
rips out a foetus for sacrifice high on a smouldering altar.
Now she has need of a fierce, cruel ghost in her work — so she makes one:
nothing is easier. All death pleases her, serving her purpose.
Plucking the bloom from a bairn's pink cheeks: so; leaving a taint: so;
snipping a lock of a dying youth's hair with her sinister hand: so.
Often at funerals, even of kinsmen, she'll pass for a mourner,
brooding, embracing the corpse as if fussing and kissing a loved one —
only to bite down, maiming the face; force open the dead mouth,
working the jaw loose; bite off the tongue that has stuck to the dry throat,
whispering horrors and murmuring secrets between the cold lips,
pouring in mumbles, despatching reports to the listening dead souls.

THE DISCOVERER'S MAN

His handkerchief, a pin or coin he'd touched,
a button from his shirt, a feather caught
on his coattail — such tokens would fetch a price...
Men came to shake his hand, or rub their warts
upon his famous skin; young mothers held
babies for him to bless with luck or wisdom —
could he ward off the pox? — while others pressed
bribes for the questions they would have him ask.
One woman, facing down a blush, gave him
a scrap of cloth, and asked that he get blood on it:
she would return next day to pay him
if he would care to nominate a fee...?
Blood of a witch! Can you believe such a thing?
I think you may be worldly after all.

Boy that I was, I can only guess
at what he must have made of me; and he,
tricked out in a high-crowned hat, Geneva cape,
staff, spurs, and bucket-top boots — he might have been
a landed squire or country magistrate...
You think us credulous? Of course you do.
So young, so quick to judge! Friend, these were days
of comets in the air, various auguries,
marvellous tempests, sights on the sea —
that we might have a witch nested among us
was not the strangest news we heard.
Proceedings would begin at dawn, he said.
Next day we found ourselves at the chapel house
uncertain who had summoned whom.

It fell to me (though *why* is more than I can say:
I had not then addressed a congregation)
to tell how, ever since her husband's death,
Old Bess had shunned society; how week on week
her vacant place in church would be remarked;
how she had made a stranger of herself
so long that when she turned to her next neighbour,
begging a bowl of curds, she was denied;
how she cursed him for this; and how his child
sickened and died soon afterwards. I took my seat
light-headed among murmurs of approval,
part of the crowd once more, strange to myself
for all my eloquence, and some three-and-ninety
witnesses rose to give their evidence…

But then: 'Ask not what mercy justice can afford
until, as civil law requires, you hear
the witch condemned out of her own mouth.' So:
officers must be sent to search her home —
he called it ten to one that they would find
trinkets such as beads or crucifixes
or other trumpery; meantime she must be stripped
and should the devil's marks be found about her
(sure enough, two bitch's teats hung down
between her secrets and the fundament)
then she must be kept from sleep and meat
and watched most constantly.
                              Old Bess confessed
at first light on the third day. He seized on me
to write her testimony:

> *On First of May,*
> *Year of Our Lord Sixteen Forty-Five,*
> *Elizabeth Bell confessed she kept Familiars*

including, but not restricted to, a Greyhound
called Vinegar Tom, a Ferret by the name
of Littleman, a Shrew called Peck-in-the-Crown,
and also a most verminous Mouse called News;
and having summoned up and suckled them
she sent her Imps to spread the Dropsy, and to kill
Richard Tayler's Horse and Michael Edwards's Swine.
And freely she confessed to having met
all hugger-mugger with divers adjacent
Witches in other Towns (we took their names)
who caused the Justice's son to stray and drown
in the Sea-marshes God have Mercy.

He took me by the arm: we stepped outside.
The magistrates were due within the hour.
Bell's list of names would carry him through Essex
to Suffolk, Norfolk, Kent and Bedfordshire —
might it please me to accompany him as scribe?
The wages would be modest, but I could expect
to witness many true and strange effects:
he had himself observed a Kentish woman
who mothered lambs; and once, contrariwise,
had seen a goat delivered of a human shape —
evil rambled among us! England was plagued
with Satan's emissaries! We must pluck them down
and let the good news be proclaimed in smoke.
'Such names,' he said, 'no mortal could invent.'

Touch a needle: watch it scent about,
quivering after its true north, uncertain,
not to be trusted till it settle — such was I.
God knows, a man's life has few turning points —
say he forsakes his father's dearest hope
to answer his vocation; or say he marries

for love, so losing his inheritance:
do such acts constitute a free election?
Look to yourself: how many decisions brought
you to this parish, minister-to-be?
Fewer than you might care to think!
We are as we were made. But standing there
holding the widow's words in my two hands
I knew chance had at last combined with choice.

That evening, waiting in the middle wood
for Alice to appear, I turned it over:
whether to sell, with scant words and poor sighs,
her dearly-bought affections; whether to leave her
suddenly on what must seem a fool's errand…
There was a stand of laurel we had made
our meeting place; I had prepared some words
that balanced a worldly wish to prove myself
against my promise to make Alice my wife.
I sat, then stood and paced about, then sat
once more. Then lay and studied stalks and blades.
Then thought to pass the time by picking simples
for a posy that might sweeten our farewell;
but, bending to my task, disturbed a woodlark's nest.

The buzz and fluster of a woodlark's flight —
scissor and stitch at once! I followed his swerve
north where the woods run out to open fields
and the coal path spools down to the harbour — there
I lost him. Where was Alice? I looked out
over meadows yet to be laid up for mowing,
ponds and cherry orchards. Hedgerows lined
the road I meant to climb next day.
How paltry my equivocations seemed,
and how unmanly, how unmannerly,

to stay and parcel out my reasons,
such that I could not ask her to allow,
much less approve… Better to leave at once.
I met with him at dawn. We headed east.

They say there is a bird, the osprey, the fish-hawk,
so majestic it can mesmerise
its prey, subduing it without a touch:
a fair example of authority.
But whether, as the book says, the firmament
'sheweth the handiwork of the Creator'
(who 'sets a tabernacle for the sun'
which is a 'strong man coming from his chamber,
friend to the bridegroom,' yes?) was all one to him.
Not that he had a narrow nature, not
that he made a painful study of his life;
but I marvel that his mind could entertain
nothing but proven truths that, being few,
huddled together like beasts in a storm.

Yet he was merciful, and stood upon these points:
that *we* should not accuse another soul
nor force confession from the examinate
by violence. Our methods must be nice.
Sometimes to keep them waking was enough —
if they would sit or offer to couch down
we would desire them to walk about —
and the swimming test was only used
at such time of the year as when none took
a harm by it. The man was so averse
to witnessing a spectacle of pain
that when our work was done he would not suffer us
to tarry long or watch the execution;
how can you call him, as is the fashion, cruel?

Cruel. You say as much, the way you shift
and smile, and study the rugosity
of the damson stones you've ranged about your plate —
your very attitude accuses us!
And still you smile. Well, I shall take your part.
You think our evidence the product of
ill-disposed constitutions, silly souls
whose fancies, working by gross fumes and vapours,
led them to believe themselves such people
as their confessions blazoned them to be;
as for the Discoverer, as for me, why,
you judge us *busy men* as I suppose,
troublesome fellows out for gain, or else
frighted by devils of our own design —

am I not right? Ah, child! Had you but seen
the welcome and good entertainment we received
ranging from town to town without control,
when his name ran on ahead like hope itself
pausing to wait for us at a turn in the road
or on a stranger's lips… to have but heard
a crowd of russet-coats imploring us
to such alms-deeds, such tender ministries…
well. Unrecorded is not unremembered.
One night (now, were my goodwife still alive
I would not speak of this! And this but one
example drawn from many: I tell it
in confidence that you will keep it close),
one night, I say, a *girl* stole to my room.

She was, she said, with child (and showing signs),
her first, she said (as I could well believe
for she was barely more than child herself),
and having neither mother, sister, nor

any female companion, and being much afraid
of what her father, should he find her changed,
might do, had come to me. In brief
she was affected by a strange disease:
and now, before I well know what is happening,
she has untied a ribbon, pulled down her blouse,
and shown herself — her pale skin lapped by candlelight,
butter-gold, flawless; except her breasts were dappled
here and there with grey-green blemishes — and she:
'Might these be fairy rings? Am I bewitched?'

I stood aghast like you, helpless and mute —
she takes my hand — her breath on me, her bright
eyes on me all this time — and draws me near
until, as a flower at the end of day
closes upon a raindrop, my fingers close
upon her trembling warmth… But — one more glass,
sir, one more glass of wine before you go!
Now, I insist: the parish will be yours
tomorrow. God and his people will forgive
a little cheer… Suppose you sit once more —
why, yes, there if you like, where you can see
my herb garden… I planted it the year
dear Alice passed: in summer you will wake and drowse
to delicate perfumes… A glass I say!

There. Now let me beg your further judgement.
I mean John Knowles. You must have heard the name —
he was notorious even in his youth
when he was summoned, twice, before the synod.
Pastor of Brandeston? That was his title,
though if he sought to make a fair show in the flesh
such is the devil's business! An old man?
Certain as I am I, but young enough

to play the knave with us, making us run
him back and forth three nights and days together
before he would confess to having sunk
a sailing vessel out of Ipswich… and yet
when it came (after much wrestling,
not to begrudge our toil) the fall was swift.

Drag a man from his last-but-one defence —
and then stand down. Have patience. He will yield.
Permit his vanity one bauble — he is apt
to cast it back at you, for pride achieves
its final flower in authoring its own
defeat. I say his was a free confession.
*Did it not grieve you to have made
fourteen new widows in a quarter-hour?*
(I waited his reply.) No, he was joyful
to see the power his imps possessed.
Did you not fear the gallows or the stake?
No, for he had a charm to keep him free.
And do you now repent your wickedness?
No. Cruel malice was his chief delight.

His was the only execution that we witnessed.
Before he was brought out, they cut his tongue
('We must have no more juggling from you, John')
and stripped him to his shirt. They fastened him
with shackles and a steel brace to the stake
and hung a bag of powder round his neck.
Then officers stacked reed and faggots
about his body, and set fire on the reed —
the wind being high, this took no little time —
and as I was so jostled in the press
I saw no more until a great flame rose
(the crowd fell silent then) that sparkled and deformed

the visor of his face — and so at last
the powder caught, and he gave up the ghost.

How enviously life clings to its toy
and then casts it aside! Broiled black, puffed up,
Knowles suffered great extremity in his death,
which notwithstanding he had borne with patience —
and it seemed the people were impressed by this
for as they went their ways some doffed their hats,
causing my companion to cry out
that Knowles was scandalous, that he had carried himself
as though he were the holy sacrament
even unto the stake, and that they had
done right to send the wolf back whence he came;
and while he spoke, I noted his pale brow
and the unseasonable bloom upon his cheeks,
for these were signs. He died within the year.

Know this: the instrument whereby God called
so many to knowledge, so many to salvation;
the man of letters that readily could give
in any matter of controversy
a godly learned sentence; the man of law
who persecuted in excess of two
hundred and fifty witches — of whom more
than half were duly executed — passed
peacefully in his bed of a consumption,
not greatly troubled in his conscience as
you may have falsely heard, nor was he once
suspected. And with great zeal he went about
his godly work some two years unmolested
until the Lord in mercy gave him rest.

I tried to see a life continuing the trade,
taking our method north through Lincolnshire,
perhaps to Scotland where the savages
busied themselves designing ever crueller tortures —
was this my mission? To enlighten them? —
but no: I made for home with tales to tell,
took up my father's ministry and in time
persuaded Alice to forgive my leaving her.
Some discoverers, seeking to be justified,
have published tedious apologies,
but such comes too near tendering a confession.
Our sanction may be found in the Book of Exodus
twenty two, eighteen. I have committed
(and need commit) nothing further to record.

What comes back now most clearly, and most often,
is not the tidy, disembellished funeral
(he wanted neither psalms nor solemn bells,
no rosemary to ornament his coffin),
much less my undeniable disappointment
at learning that he was — not quite *low-born*,
yet something shy of a true gentleman — like me
a minister's third son (and his mother French!
She had escaped, he said, the massacres in Paris);
but walking out together that first morning,
our work before us, when we found the verges lit
with new-blown colours — bluebells, cornflowers, eyebright —
like intermeddling voices, so I thought,
each one contending with its neighbour to be heard.

My companion walked in silence.
(Hours would pass before I found the nerve
to enquire towards what his silence tended,
and when at last I did, his answer was so short and quick —

'The days to come' — I did not ask again.)
The sun dazzled my eyes, and I allowed myself
to fancy we had left the road behind
and were ascending into the blue ether,
England disappearing far below.
Already the syringa was in bloom,
its scent so concentrated in the dawn —
open the window: this herb, breathe it now:
the smell is like the sweat of a young girl
who runs in a summer meadow, is it not?

THE FOOTNOTE
23–24 October 1642

Sir Adrian Scrope
deserves the footnote
he always gets:

cut down at smokefall
on the field at Edgehill,
found & stripped

according to custom,
that night the frost
stanches his bleeding;

at dawn he wakes
starved with cold
in a mass of bodies —

nobles, tapsters —
all of them naked,
no way to know

who's who, which which,
so he pulls a corpse
or three about him

as you might tug
your blanket up
about your ears,

roll over cosy in
your bed to face
the wall night-night —

SEATED FIGURE WITH ARMS RAISED

Early reports suggest
an innocent bystander
picked out of the crowd —
his unreadable face,
the bare detail of that wrist
straining to right itself
as he shields his eyes,
at pains to make us out —
but of course, on rolling news
nobody would trust
a changeable account
from an undisclosed source
of questionable intent —
and just as well because

later reports insist
that with a trained eye
it's possible to discern
through the protective screen
a device upon his chest
proving the man's a stray
from the ragtag band
caught out in a firestorm —
but of course, on rolling news
this too might turn around:
that could be a uniform;
he could be one of ours;
those arms could be raised
in victory or surrender —

and further reports exist
claiming the man as
martyr or civilian;
the thing itself or just
the raw material;
war criminal,
collateral,
gist, pith, gloss —
could be we'll never know
what he would make of us,
how things are looking now
from his side of the screen —
the story isn't done:
this one will run and run

THE CURLEW

Sighs & groans. As it crawls to a standstill
the train becomes a fortress.

Outside: pitiless silence. Emptied sky.
Snowbound farms. Ever-deepening blue.

The vulnerable economies of owl & fox.
Fields brushed, as by a comet's tail, with winter.

No announcement. No sign of the guard.
We have reached the threshold, it is everywhere at once

in depthless white drifts unbroken
to the world's rim: Everyman's harvest...

I close my eyes. An automated voice declares
a range of light snacks is available. It's airless —

scumfish — as the hide at Clara Vale —
the Primus stove, the stash of second earlies,

and who is this if not mine own George Fox
(for by his leathern trews I know him)

twirling the logbook on its string,
actual, talked-up, talking

in lines skimmed from his Penguin Classics *Journal*
where it rests in my hands: *I had forsaken all*

the priests, for there was none that spoke to my condition...
The world seemed but a briary wilderness

beset with men's inventions: windy doctrines
blowed folk about now this way and now that

from sect to sect — O here were wells
without water, here was the cloud without rain!

From Clara Vale to Firbank Fell,
Dirt Pot to Sparty Lea,

my dream tour of hilltop outposts
where Quakers & hare-eyed Methodists dug in

for the love of clarity
high on the law, and the promise of salvation

abstracted in varieties of silence
above all. Friendly people

who *would not come into no great towns*
but lived in the fells like butterflies

numbering sins
clean as tumblestones, finding fences

where others saw open fields,
their inward light a sullen joy

in sun-slashed verticals, Irish weather
driving across the uplands, and the rained-out

curlew's sob that might have been
a true saying: *Be as a stranger unto all.*

III

BRANTWOOD SENILIA

In heaven I mean to go and talk to Pythagoras and Socrates and Valerius Publicola. I shan't care a bit for Rosie there, she needn't think it. What will grey eyes and red cheeks be good for there?
— John Ruskin, letter to Susan Beever, from Assisi, Sacristan's Cell (25 June 1874)

To-day, being my sixty-first birthday, I would ask leave to say a few words to the friends who care for me, and the readers who are anxious about me, touching the above-named illness itself. For a physician's estimate of it, indeed, I can only refer them to my physicians. But there were some conditions of it which I knew better than they could: namely, first, the precise and sharp distinction between the state of morbid inflammation of brain which gave rise to false visions (whether in sleep, or trance, or waking, in broad daylight, with perfect knowledge of the real things in the room, while yet I saw others that were not there), and the not morbid, however dangerous, states of more or less excited temper, and too much quickened thought, which gradually led up to the illness, accelerating in action during the eight or ten days preceding the actual giving way of the brain...
— John Ruskin, *Fors Clavigera* Letter 88 (8 February 1880)

Too fast and far again! by much; the impetus of phrase running away with me.
— John Ruskin, additional note no. 54 to *Modern Painters* Vol.2 (1883 revised ed.)

My dear little birds,
before me on my desk this morning
where I sit preparing tomorrow's lesson
    lies a copy of *The Witches' Rout* by Agostino de' Musi —
        Agostino Veneziano your teachers will call him —
wherein a carriage made of dragon bones
~~and drawn by two naked figures~~
    is depicted making topsy-turvy progress through a jungle
scattering goats & geese & winged skeletal reptiles
    and there, look now, there atop it all the witch squats
    ~~as one at stool~~ — manly forearm,
muscular shoulder, *pendulis mammis* —
                ~~the narrow dugs it is~~
                ~~her business to possess~~ —
filthy hair streaming *contra naturam*
    out in a headwind of mephitic vapours…
        Time out of mind such creatures have impressed
the dreams of those who live, as it were, by watchfires,
fearful of neighbours, fearful that the law
they hammered into whatsoever shape as pleased them
may yet prove versatile —
    their sensual rites & ceremonies,
    novelties & conceits;
    their pharisaical holiness… —
and this is but a scholar's imitation you will say, rude work
though of a fine school — a fine school be it allowed, and good enough
to lose itself beside the master's —
        & yet
        & yet

        steady the hand that hovers over
                the acid-bitten cliché
        steady the elbow

behind this
engraving on paper

Fro spot my spyryt þer sprang in space

so now

*Piazza Sta Maria del Pianto, Rome (1840). A pensive study of
old clothes sun-sipped dry in the Jews' quarter, hanging out of a
marble architrave smashed & built into a piece of Roman frieze
mouldering into broken brickwork projected over wooden windows
propped on grey entablature. A vestige of yet-legible inscription:*
NOMINE FORTUNA. *No important lines, no beauty of object.
A pendent hodgepodge of contrasted feeling cheese-caked into
picturesque febrility. An episode. A grief in, as it were, parenthesis.
A match without a marriage, as after news of an engagement. A
church embedded sans façade among the common sort of houses. A
succour from St Peter's mere bewilderment & worry. Graphite
heightened w/ touches of white body colour on grey-green paper.*

Beresford Chapel, Walworth: a bare, oblong,
low-ceilinged barn, each brick-arched window filled
with small-paned glass requiring iron bars
threaded like halves of cobweb to stay true.
No traceries, no clustered shafts, no vaulting.
No fantasies. No perpendicular flights
of aspiration. Clean lines, and severe.
Pews shut-in with partitions of plain deal
and neatly brass-hatched doors. No pulpit, merely
a stout, four-legged box of well-grained wainscot,
but decorated with a velvet cushion —
crimson, with golden tassels at the corners —
which formed my one resource, for when I tired
of Dr Andrews's sermon I could watch

the colours texturing the folds & creases
each time he thumped it. Beresford. That's where
we worshipped: Papa, Mama, and I.
Poor preparation, this, for Rouen! Rouen
wardered by groups of solemn statuary
clasped by stems of sculpted leafage crowned
by fretted niche & fairy pediment
like inextricably meshed gossamer;
Rouen with her surge & foam of pious chivalry
breaking on crystal cliffs to stand revealed
as every hidden thing shall be, insatiable at prayer
or pillage, lending grace to English rudeness,
venom to Italy's cunning... Rouen with all
her avarice & intricacies, gargoyles
open-mawed, molten, drenching ornament
down spires vertiginously pinnacled —
insanae substructiones! Inutiles domos! —
yet piping pastoral songs of innocence —

The Palazzo Contarini-Fasan, Venice (1841). Higgledy terraced
structures the colours of ice creams & sorbets w/ no bland tinting.
No calligraphic decoration. Graphite, watercolour & body colour. A
thorough spell in the vernacular. Stone filigree spidering rhythmic
tessellations w/ some scratching out. Details that become a refuge.
Detail that becomes a refuge. A long-drawn replica in which new
life may even now be in the offing. A sulky grandeur, by the bye.
A naughty jailer. A determined postulant. A barber-pole mooring
post. A dipped oar tilting for trouble. The Doge's tottering state
stepping off on grey paper.

Worn somewhat, and not a little weary,
Sandro's uncommon Fortitude, in this
his first recorded work. Consider it
a moment, if you please, before you pass
hurriedly on to see The Birth of Venus
next door, and notice that Sandro began
where you perhaps will end: with weariness.
Would you have guessed that Fortitude allows
(allows? approves of!) reverie? See how
her fingers play in restless idleness
or nervousness about her sword hilt
(sword or mace? I've lost my notes about her...).
She is no match, it may be, for the trials
that are to come, yet see her armour shine
in readiness, her gentle fingers apt
to grip her sword (or mace) should she be called.
Lips pursed and eyes averted, she has smiled,
and not a little ruefully, at her fate
from time to time. She has no smile today.
Her quality must be borne day-long, life-long.
To flaunt it ever is not to possess
it quite. See Pollaiolo's Virtues pose
and attitudinise: thus they perform
their various meanings. Fortitude must
contain — must *be* — all that she stands for. Go,
see whatever the Uffizi has
to tempt you; but remember Fortitude
whose battle did not begin today,
nor yesterday, nor on the Sunday last.
Many a day has passed since it began.
They are so wedded to their righteousness,
those lesser Virtues, quite incapable
of being tempted. They would not dare risk
complacency. She would be lost without it.

But sword or mace? Go now. It is no matter.
I will not need you until tomorrow morning.

Ravine at Maglans (1849?). Deeper brown on brown. A limestone precipice stepped with horizontal cleavages to overlook the void. No water but a dream of water years back, far down, running harum-scarum strong enough to turn a mill. A spate become a thread. A visit out of season. A torrent bed of what must have been snow-melt now entirely dry. No stones crumble but flow, subside, rhythmic as cloud, as high-built, as unsubstantial over the long haul. Quartz strips ribboning a treed crevasse fringed w/ curled & unfurled fronds. Leaves shook to palsy by the noon wind's spite. A rock fissured. A great fault. A graphite rock fissured in brown ink & ink wash heightened w/ flesh-toned body colour on white paper.

Last night St Ursula sent me her dianthus
out of her bedroom window, with her love —
living dianthus, and a single dried
sprig of her other window flower, vervain…
How many flowers are named in *Genesis*?
Good answer! Not one. Plenty of trees, however.
It was a poet planted flowerbeds
that Eden might be filled with tremulous,
frivolous petals — I dare say he was right,
they were made to be noticed! And to see
a poppy husk fall from a bursting flower
is to know something of the life to come
once the body has turned to dust & ashes,
even as our dying breath aspires
towards our Father's house… As for the trees,
what can we learn of noble constancy
more than we find in the pure laurel leaf,
so numerable, so sequent and serene?

~~open the envelope~~
~~petals & may~~
~~spill on the table~~
~~where I remain~~
~~preparing the lesson~~

~~bruise-edged rose petals~~
~~cling to my fingers~~
~~dust-motes dancing~~
~~gnats in a sun-shaft~~
~~myrrh, or a snuffbox?~~

~~write to me, tell me~~
~~who do you dance with~~
~~oftenest, often?~~
~~grey eyes & red cheeks~~
~~useless in heaven~~

~~undowered, garlanded~~
~~with no forget-me-nots:~~
~~compassed about~~
~~with the forgetfulness~~
~~of all the world~~

~~honour unwon~~
~~kind words unsaid~~
~~good deeds undone:~~
~~none of these, none~~
~~touch me more nearly~~

Now, if I say 'St Ursula has sent me
a pot of pinks!' ~~some will say I have gone~~
~~heartily, headily mad, but~~ all it means
is that the flowers I received of late

(from the hand of whatsoever friend or stranger)
helped greatly in my work, and afterwards
reproved me in their own way for its failure.
~~But how much love of mine have others lost~~
~~because one poor sick child would not receive~~
~~the part of love that yet belongs to her!~~
Think now, sweet milkmaids of Albion
whose face is your fortune, think of one
lying still there, nearly a skeleton,
and ask yourselves: *We have a little sister*
and she has no breasts: what shall we do for our sister
in the day of her espousals?

South Side of the Basilica of St. Mark's, Venice, from the Loggia of
the Ducal Palace (c.1851). An eerie vantage. A capricious helter-
skelter variety of application, quickening details of watercolour
passing for time-veined marble scaled-up from a daguerrotype. An
echo's volume. Shadows lilt & flourish over chessboard floortiles. A
kind of hectic colour. Disallowance of perspective. Sculpted relief
without recession. Megrims & mysteries; conceits & divertisements.
The uncapped St Jean d'Acre's pillar giving on to the southern
portico. A Byzantine capital. A sonata on a virginal. Graphite &
watercolour heightened w/ white on three jointed pieces of paper.

Up my spirit leapt, so glad
to shed this gross flesh and have done!
My ghost, given up by the grace of God,
was led where marvels are counted common.
I climbed to where cliff-top meets cloud —
vertiginous heights no man has known —
my soul drawn on towards a wood
decked with countless jewels & stones.
It is hard to credit a sight so fine
as the wash of light in which they shone:

woman never wove a gown
so dearly adorned, so lit with splendour.

In splendour, cliffs of crystal stood
crisp as ice, clear & clean.
At their foot, a forest spread:
the trees were touched with a red-blue sheen
and leaves of burnished silver slid
quivering to & fro between
limbs that shimmered like blue jade
each time a light-gleam touched the scene.
The gravel underfoot was strewn
with gems, and the sun seemed quite outshone
by those precious, oriental stones
so dearly adorned, so lit with splendour.

The splendour of the grove was such
that my grief left me — it lifted clear;
the fragrance of the fruit so fresh,
I found I needed no other fare.
Birds flew together, branch to branch
like flecks of flame — now here now there;
no human symphony can match,
nor voice nor string delight the ear
with such a song: they blessed the air
with a sweet accord that swooned & shone
with harmonies you will never hear
but there where all is lit with splendour.

So adorned in splendour was
that forest where I met my fate,
a cunning man could not devise
a fitting way to tell of it.
Climbing pear trees, apple trees;

browsing wonders — pretty sport!
And soon the flowers & fields & hedgerows
turned beautifully intricate
with burns & water gardens. Bright
as burnished gold the fellside shone
where I trailed a stream that ran with light,
dearly adorned & lit with splendour.

But a greater splendour was yet to come:
a riverbank of beryl ablaze
where water swept & swirled in a foam
of hurrying murmurs & confused airs.
The stream bed glinted with a gleam
like sunlight filtered through stained glass
or winter starlight, when it may seem
we're all alone when the clouds pass.
Each pebble bright as Hesperus:
sapphire, emerald — each one shone
with a light too bright for similes,
dearly adorned & lit with splendour.

Study of Gneiss Rock, Glenfinlas (1853–54). A living witness. A verticality more smooth than the water over wch it rears. Glib-channelled water rushing; dry rock dripping — fluid, labial rock, less still than the wildflowers & feathered grasses that cling in unguessed cracks & overhang. Mapped lichens. Lampblack, body colour. A cumbrous slab. An unobtrusive majesty. A happenstance long sought before seen, loved long before understood. A lesson of devotion to be found always, found but once. An obstinacy gladdened by the river's flux, the ice floe's pluck & laving. Pen & ink over graphite on wove paper w/ some scratching out.

In Santa Croce, Florence, here we are
well quit of restoration, for who cares
about this slab with its poor bit of sculpture?
An old man in the deeply-folded cap
worn by the city's scholars & gentlemen
c.1300–1500, dead,
a book upon his breast, and over it
his hands lie folded. At his feet, the legend:

TEMPORIBVS HIC SVIS PHYLOSOPYE
ATQ MEDICINE CVLMEN FVIT ET MAGISTER
GALILEVS DEGALILEIS OLIM BONAIVTIS QVI
ETIAM SVMMO INMAGISTRATV MIRO
QVODAM MODO REM PVBLICAM DILEXIT
CVIVS SANCTE MEMORIE BENE ACTE

The worn face, still the old man's perfect portrait —
though one struck out by a master's chisel
at a venture, just so, with a few rough touches;
the falling drapery of his citizen's cap
beyond description, with the choice of folds
exquisite in its ornamental pattern;
the carpet he lies on almost uninjured,
elaborate with fringe & frond
relieving the severity of the figure…
and see now, see how the cushion's nearly-perfect tassels
balance to fill the angles of the stone —

*Study of a Peacock's Breast Feather (1873?). A single plume,
painted of its natural size. One iridescent throb transitioning from
the active plume's obliquity to the decorative's dualled symmetry.
An uncertain correspondence w/ a heart-shaped flower petal. A
cold thrill: a pang as of a nice deep wasp sting. Moss green moving
via jade to emerald, indigo to lapis lazuli: as much as is allowed,*

having neither hocus-pocus nor heaven to dip a brush in. An heraldic emblem;
watch & ward against incipient commodity. A lost key to a blue box for blue
girls w/ grey eyes. Watercolour & body colour on paper.

      whirrrrrrr-r-r-r-r-r-r
     pink! pink! pink! cherry-erry-erry
   pew-pew-pew-pew-poor-pew-pew
The chaffinches chirp but feebly; this June snow
    discomposes them
                  Coniston
  bright as glass
      ill-cast
  by an undiscerning hand
         wave-lines
  showing like flaws in planes of fine crystal

 unsteady, unstill
 troubling & troubled

  What is it droppeth as the gentle rain from heaven?
   Child, according to this morning's *Spectator*
'tis nothing but the filtration of money from above downwards —
  an oft-observed phenomenon
        concessum propter duritiem cordis
                 a thing allowed
    and properly recorded in our holy book of double entry
I mean St Usura's *Gospel of Filth*
    wherein we learn his doctrine of arithmetic
               that $2 + 2 = 5$...
        O we are so humane,
           forsooth, we are so wise,
         that whereas our ancestors had tar barrels for witches
         we have them for everybody else —
        and we will have our cauldrons cooled, please Hecate,

after Mr Darwin's theory
with baboon blood!
Occulted by daylight
we will drive the witches' trade ourselves
as, once, I saw a boy with his basket of rotten figs
poor little costermonger
before the south façade of the Ducal Palace
stooping to cry *Fighiaie! Fighiaie!*
Inibito a chiunque il vendere frutti cattivi
19th June, 1516
(i.e. before that nobody thought of doing so)
~~as, more than once, I have seen the girls at the windows: poor girls~~
~~at the windows, in the alleyways,~~
~~in the slums by the Euston Hotel, by the railway lines,~~
~~take Camden Rd towards the canal basin, lift your eyes,~~
~~do but lift your eyes as you leave the hall, gentlemen,~~
~~and you will mark them, they hold themselves~~
~~liberally, knowing our likings, poor girls, nothing to sell~~
~~but everything; nothing to sell~~
~~but themselves~~ I dewyne,
fordolked of luf-daungere too fast & far,
boiled to rags by morbid violence — No
they cannot touch me for coyning
me so misby — so misby — so misby
me wish me was a clergyman
tellin lies all day
& Flint — & Tukup — & But —
cujus sancte memorie
those rich-left heirs
Fighiaie!

O Love,
    sane as the proud flesh
        about a healing wound
            in the side of my nation

that yet may pass
    at a crisis
        into morbific substance,
            let this man work.

O Love,
    give us work
        and set us to it,
            for we are corrigible:

O fettle us
    for we are not
        after all entirely corrigible
            & stay our hand

when we would set our soul upon a cast:
teach us how to give & hazard all
we hath upon your coming, for the soul
cannot be bargained otherwise — only lost.
Impregnable to our economies
whatever the deceiver promises,
the soul is not for sale. And now, the cost
        diligently accounted for, the sum
        entered in the ledger, see this bound
        and shelved in sequence where it may be found
        by any who enquire, should any come...

    Love sets no term. Love schedules its appearances
    according to no clock of ours:

to moon-bewildered waves we each of us receive
our summons, unreluctant. Let walk upon them
all who can.

                        …came Phaedra then, and Procris,
              next Ariadnè, fairest of all Minos' daughters,
                      whose daddy's mind was a slaughterhouse
              bright Ariadnè
              whom Theseus once from Crete
              to the tilled acres of sacred Athens led —
              nor had he the joy of her, his heart's desire,
              poor Ariadnè
              fair, moon-bewildered —
                        false Dionȳsus witnessed against her;
                        Artĕmis slew her…

      O, feed her with apricocks & dewberries,
      with purple grapes, green figs & mulberries

Is she not with me here among the hawthorn blossom?

    Diodati, a year with no summer,
        and the world was void —
            þe fyrre in þe fryth
                — she was the Universe

                      At dusk
pipistrelles flit like black rags torn at the edges
    bonfire cinders
    riding the vortex
    spiralling circuits
    all round the terrace
    all day have I sat here
    preparing the lesson

My dear little birds, did you not see the gleam of sunshine yesterday?

Hadst thou but seen her in it
   bareheaded, barefoot
between the laurels & the primrose bank

Moss & Wild Strawberry (1873). Gentle, hesitant line. A suggestion in the genitive. A secret in midsummer. A slackening deft moss nested in cleaved stone. Traces of body colour on grey-blue paper trefoiled w/ dewy sequins. Seekings. Rooting a declivity in the rock revealed now by a berry's posture. A gaze darkening where lines triangulate palely. A beckoning. A suggestive gesture.

IV

THE MARBLE VEIL

This unfamiliar place, if we succeed in figuring out what's going on, could be the locus of a secret. And it might, assuming that's the case, then convey certain things, things we cannot control, things that are fatal, voluntarily uncontrolled. We need to find a compromise between what we control and what we provoke.
— Jean Nouvel

*What hides in darkness and what truths
it veils.*
— Andrew Crozier

o

That some things are lost
    some occluded

And of whether these categories are discrete
or if one may be solved in the other —

That loss may be a form
    whose element is time

That, in time, questions of loss
become questions of faith

as one passing through Ca' Rezzonico
Museo del Settecento — the city in decline
      already, the great dream
  turning lucid, eyelids trembling, the lagoon
picking up natural light — may pause
      before *Dama Velata*:
  Antonio Corradini's
marble bust of Purity
      depicted
  according to convention
as a young woman
      but (this is new) with her face covered,
  the veil a device
to show the artist's skill
      at rendering fluency in stone —
  urge to touch & try its
I want to say ductility;
      ductile: might have meant easily led
  but doesn't — so it appears to stream
down her forehead & nose,
      sweeping to gather
  at her right shoulder, hang more loose
upon her left, edges embroidered
      with a homely button pattern drawn
  across her breast
al cielo e al tempo…
      A marble veil. Corradini's specialty.

II

> *These are the hidden sayings*
> *that the living Yeshua spoke*
> > *and Yehuda Toma the twin recorded...*
> so it begins.
> Hidden sayings: *enshaje ethep* (Coptic)
> > *ethep*: hidden/secret/obscure —
> translators must choose.
> *...the scholars have taken the keys of knowledge*
> > *and have hidden them...*
> > *There is nothing hidden that will not be revealed...*
> The translator has chosen.
> > That some things are better seen
> obscured — that's veil logic for you.
> That it is the wish for clarity
> > distorts? Veil logic.
> Some things are lost
> according to convention. Is
> > *Dama Velata*'s face occluded
> or lost for good? Lost, I'd say,
> supposing it exists, but things get through:
> > beauty — absolute: conventional —
> and that her hair is plaited, and that her eyes
> are closed — not downcast: closed
> > as in reverie.
> *Nothing that is hidden is lost,*
> *but at the same time nothing that is found*
> > *is absolutely new...*

flickering candescence —
phosphors vexed livid
            like sun-dazzle on choppy waters…
        silence — primed, held —
then light once more shook out to flare
                taut as a wind-snapped sheet on a clothesline…
        in the small hours
creeping to wake you
            that we both might
        witness the revelation:
the flashbulb-lit marbling of cloud amphitheatres,
            it was ours
        ours for a moment —
almost we could have read by that light
            but what would we have read
        my head in your lap
both of us looking out over
                crazed rooftops, terraces
        chimneypots, aerials
shuttered windows, bell towers
            the tessellated congeries of the Dorsoduro skyline
        stuccoed façades
courtyard an orchestra pit open below us —
            il lampo che candisce
        alberi e muri e li sorprende in quella
eternità d'istante, something like that,
                strana sorella?

IV

or 'The Aspern Papers',
the great, terrible bit where Miss Bordereau
        appears at our man's shoulder
    just as he is about to pilfer —
so he reckons —
        her long-dead lover's letters,
    the green shade lifted from her eyes once & for all
(that she is blind has only just been revealed —
        her niece, incredulous, asking the narrator
    Do you think she can see?)
and then: *there in her nightdress,*
        in the doorway of her room…
    her hands were raised,
she had lifted the everlasting curtain
        that covered half her face,
    and for the first, the last,
the only time I beheld her extraordinary eyes.
        They glared at me, they made me
    horribly ashamed….
I went toward her, to tell her I meant no harm.
        She waved me off with her old hands,
    retreating before me
in horror… next thing I knew she had fallen back
        with a quick spasm, as if
    death had descended on her…
Unforgettable — except
        I'd managed to forget.

but none of the five sacred facts
concerning Giorgioni help
   with *La Tempesta*
  or, as it appears in the Gallerie dell'Accademia,
La Zingarella e il Soldato
   though surely that is Eve —
  sullen, imperfectly rendered,
right leg dislocated —
   giving Cain suck — *These nursing babies*
  are like those who enter the kingdom… —
Adam looking on, proud, contrapposto,
   propped on his staff, dressed up
  like a soldier in his cutaway crimson jacket…
You were ready; I was not. Early days
   and our illustrious progenitors
  oblivious to the rebuke
that jags the sky
   above Castelfranco, the city walls
  emblazoned with the Carraresi coat of arms —
A city built upon a high hill & fortified
   cannot fall,
  nor can it be hidden;
blind, also, to the riches of the earth, the herbs of the field
   that they will work in sorrow & sweat
  all the days of their life
starting tomorrow: for the now
   all eyes are on the bairn.

and there it is again in Carducci:
A le cineree trecce alzato il velo
        verde.... A sit-down meal in Venice is
    rarely a good idea. Street food's where it's at.
Locals move at speed, head bowed, monastic.
        Bloated & self-medicated, pushing forty,
    I approach enough's enough from different angles.
Is the vineyard owner a good man
        or an usurer: *ourome enchre[sto]s*
    or *ourome enchre[ste]s*?
The restorer must choose. Either way
        his servants will be beaten, his son
    murdered either way. Cinereous,
out of puff, competing with the gargoyle
        on Santa Maria Formosa
    that so offended Ruskin...
And did Yeshua's mother give him
        life or lies?
    A century after Corradini
veiled busts were all the rage:
        for Strazza, Rossi, Monti they represented
    the soul of Italy, a secular Madonna
vanilla-bonded, a contrivance
        aiming to stir emotions maybe not
    especially deep. *Il velo verde.*
If the phrase 'green shade' occurs five times
        there must be something in it.

Not that it is historical, I mean
the Fall in *La Tempesta*, Adam & Eve
  as louche Venetians, worldly, too cool;
 it is eternal, waiting to be found
everywhere, then & now — call it
  The Soldier and the Gypsy Girl,
 call it the story of a man of letters
who dreams of being a thief
  until life makes him a gardener — a little
 green thought goes a long way.
We cannot all have our gardens now
  nor our pleasant fields
 to meditate in at eventide...
As for us, recusants for life,
  childless & at large among
 Mother Italy's crop of spoiled bambini,
our money goes on bottled water,
  pistachio gelato, faux Murano baubles,
 tickets for Damien Hirst's hot tat...
Things to see, free stuff, the Regata Storica —
  pick a colour: cheer it: green:
 why not. Should your boat win
it hardly matters. In this dream we're
  all to ourselves with love to squander like
 so much future-perfect guilt.
And they are like children
  living in a field that is not theirs...

Always all already over,
corybantic rapture, the never-achieved
        republic of promise, fantastic & involved,
    infamous pretender
eating the bread of bitterness,
        city without sound, *even the shade*
    of that which once was great is passed away.
Ruskin went to ground here, Rilke
        came to grief — on his first visit
    after the war: *You do not know, Princess,*
how altogether different the world is now...
        Whoever thinks of living as he used to
        will find himself continually caught
in the mere once-again
        and its sterility.... Ten decades on
    fascist Salvini tweets
with Trumpian scare-quotes: *"Censimento" dei Rom*
        e controllo dei soldi pubblici spesi...
    while the Madonna nods in dumb assent
wie eine Nymphe die den Zeus empfing
        and those variegated stones of Venice —
    jasper & porphyry,
serpentine spotted
        with flecks of snow, *her bluest veins to kiss —*
    lilt & dazzle
as she lifts San Giorgio like a sunstruck wineglass
        and gazes languidly into the waves.

    ten years of glory —
court sculptor, Vienna: 1.700 florins per annum
        (plus expenses) — till the fashion turns:
    begins the unending
search for a not-unreliable benefactor,
        and the trials, and the schemes, and *Vestale Velata*
    that had to be done
without a commission
        and that then never sold;
    then back to Naples for one last job: *Verità Velata*:
Veiled Truth: one final work in marble,
        a statue, a funerary ornament
    for Cecilia Gaetani dell'Aquila d'Aragona,
his patron's mother
        whose passing called for something less
    monumental — not this
embarrassment to mourning, accomplishment
        exceeding its occasion, by one
    too often overlooked, too much to prove;
or did he, Antonio Corradini, first man in Italy
        to fight for — & win — a legal distinction
    between mason & sculptor, between work & art,
think of his father
        whose prime was spent stitching
    canvas for latin-rigs on the triremes
and packing up the shrouds for the brigantines,
        such being his trade, he being a *veler*?

* * *

THE DAMNED

after Dante, Inferno, *Canto V, 121-138*

The bitterest
sorrow is not regret,
though that is part of what we suffer —
the bitterest sorrow lies in happiness rehearsed,
as when I speak of how
our fate took root.

It was a poem:
the ballad of Sir Lancelot
whom love enslaved — old fashioned stuff,
pure nonsense really, so where was the danger if
from time to time our eyes met —
where was the harm?

We read on
until we reached the line
about a kiss both looked-for and unbidden —
a kiss so long desired and yet so lightly taken —
that line was our undoing:
a sidelong

glance — another —
into each other's eyes, and we,
who since that day have never been apart,
we latecomers to everything within our hearts,
we put the book away
and read no further.

NOTES

(   )

knoop: the ground mulberry, or cloud-berry; *lop*: flea; *pew*: snow; *lea*: meadow; *plut*: to rain; *lap*: to wrap; *wite*: to blame; *tchew*: a difficult or tiresome task; *peesweep* and *peez-weep*: variations of peewit, that is, the lapwing; *keep toot*: to keep a look-out; *tup heidit*: stubborn (lit. ram-headed).

The Buttoned Lip
yem: home

Labourers, Allendale, c.1875
This poem is 'after' Edward Thomas in the sense that it is structured after Chapter 25 of *The Heart of England* (1909), which describes a couple named Robert and Margaret Page, labourers who were once farmers. *The Heart of England* is based on observations Thomas made during his wanderings across Kent, Sussex, Hampshire, Wiltshire, and Cornwall, but Chapter 25 seems to have also been influenced by lines 11-20 of John Clare's 'January' (from *The Shepherd's Calendar*), which describe a man in a tavern:

> Reading the news to mark again
> The bankrupt lists or price of grain
> Or old mores anual prophecys
> That many a theme for talk supplys
> Whose almanacks thumbd pages swarm
> Wi frost & snow & many a storm
> & wisdom gossipd from the stars
> Of politics & bloody wars
> He shakes his head & still proceeds
> Neer doubting once of what he reads

In borrowing from Thomas/Clare I've edited and changed the details freely, moving the scene to the north Pennines in the aftermath of the lead-mining industry.

biggin: building; *fornenst*: against and/or facing towards; *glim*: candle or lantern; *law*: upland; *ruddocks*: robins.

A Lyke-Wake Dirge

love darg: work done for charity; also a knitting competition in the *People's Friend* magazine.

The Matter

Non è fuggito: it is not gone. This phrase, referring to the world of the old gods, is from Pietro Metastasio (1698-1782).

The Parasite

For information about Algernon Percy (1602-68), especially in regard to his clothing, I am indebted to John Adamson's *The Noble Revolt*.

The Rogue

Henry Marten (1602–80) became MP for Berkshire in April 1640, and quickly became known for his honesty and tactlessness. These traits did not prove conducive to personal advancement. As a landowner, he was paternalistic; as a politician, he was a rebel. His position on the English presence in Ireland, for example, is astonishing. In 1642 he expressed sympathy for the Irish rebels, and compared them favourably to Charles I and his followers: "The Kings rebellion in England was farr more high then that of ye Irish rebells... much more daungerous (being within our bowells) more uniust (in that hee could not pretend to ye shaking off a yoak from his own neck...) more chargeable, & if not altogether so bloody, that is to bee imputed to Gods mercy, not to his, upon whose account must bee payed a great part even of that blood which hath bene spilt in Ireland." In August 1643, Marten overreached himself when he spoke openly in the House of Commons about deposing Charles I for the good of the country. The occasion of his comments had been the interrogation of John Saltmarsh, a puritan preacher. Marten was gaoled briefly and then 'exiled' to Berkshire; but the genie was out of the lamp and eventually so many members had addressed the question of kingship and the possibility of its forfeiture that an Act of Oblivion was introduced in 1646, striking all reference to Saltmarsh from the record. For this reason, Marten regained his seat in the House of Commons. When Charles II was crowned in 1660 there was a further Act of Oblivion, which officially absolved the parliamentarians of any wrongdoing during the civil war period, but which in practice did not preclude numerous executions and less public murders from taking place. In fact, Marten was one of the only regicides (that is, signatories of Charles I's death warrant) to avoid execution: he was imprisoned for the rest of his life — and spent time in the Tower of London, and then in gaols in Berwick-upon-Tweed and on Lindisfarne, before finally being moved to Chepstow — but his earlier defence of Sir William Davenant on the grounds that the man was too dissolute to be worthy of sacrifice may have been redeployed to save Marten's neck. In any case, Marten lived to be 78 years old, and died either of apoplexy or by choking on his supper. I am deeply indebted to Sarah Barber's scholarly biography, *A Revolutionary Rogue: Henry Marten and the English Republic* (Sutton Publishing Ltd., 2000), though the fractious relationship between Henry Marten and his brother George is my invention. Much of the second part of my poem is drawn from Marten's letters to Mary Ward. Technically, Ward was Marten's mistress, but the two lived as man and wife for much of Marten's life. Marten's letters to Ward, written from prison, were later seized by Royalists who published them in order to discredit Marten: *Coll: Henry Marten's Familiar Letters to his Lady of Delight: also Her kinde Returnes; with his Rivall R. Pettingalls Heroicall Epistles* was first published Oxford in 1662, and reprinted 1663 and 1685.

Stultorn incurate vigor malus ulcera vexat was an aphorism that Marten coined and self-applied. It can be translated as "My false industriousness worsen[ed] the wound of my foolishness". It is a play on a line from Horace's *Epistles* 1.16.24: "Stultorum incurate pudor malus ulcera celat" (The false modesty of a fool leads him to conceal his wound). *Ignavum fucos pecus a praesepibus arcent* is from Virgil's *Georgics*, IV, 168: "All, with united force, combine to drive / The lazy drones from the laborious hive" in Dryden's translation.

The Witch

Lucan (Marcus Annaeus Lucanus) was born in 39 A.D. and died in 65 A.D. In 63 A.D. he joined a group of senators conspiring to assassinate the Emperor Nero. Suetonius describes Lucan as *paene signifer*, the leader of the group. The coup failed, and Nero compelled Lucan, along with the other conspirators, to commit suicide. Lucan's *De Bello Civili* (known in English as either the *Pharsalia* or *The Civil War*) is an epic poem describing the civil war between imperial Caesar and republican Pompey, whom Lucan favours. Some have argued that Lucan constructs a republican poetic in opposition to the smooth, elevated music of Virgil, and there certainly seems to be a pointed parallel in this extract: the witch (whose name is Erichtho) is Lucan's equivalent to the Sybil of Cumae, and instead of a wise sage dispensing prophecies, Erichtho is a terrifying monster. Lucan's depiction of Erichtho's outrageous abuse of the dead may seem gratuitous, but it has a political dimension: it prefigures Caesar's behaviour after the battle at Pharsalia, when he refuses to allow the republican dead to be buried, leaving the corpses to be eaten by animals. Throughout

De Bello Civili, Caesar's lack of respect for the dead is a sign of his tyranny. In the seventeenth century, Lucan was more highly regarded than he is today, and Thomas May's translation of *De Bello Civili*, written during the English Civil War, was very popular. Both Royalist and Parliamentarian commentators drew parallels between events described in the poem and contemporary politics. In *Writing the English Republic: Poetry, Rhetoric and Politics, 1627–1660*, David Norbrook writes "A poem charged with paradox, the *Pharsalia* at once denounces civil war and incites it".

I have adapted Lucan's form, dactylic hexameter, counting stressed and unstressed syllables rather than syllable quantity or length. For the sake of rhythmic variety I have occasionally ended lines with a trochee rather than a spondee.

The Discoverer's Man

Although the characters and events in this poem are fictional, the Discoverer and his man are based loosely on Matthew Hopkins (c.1620–1647), the self-styled Witchfinder General, and John Stearne (c.1610–1670). The progress of the Discoverer mirrors that of Hopkins: the real-life Elizabeth Clarke (Hopkins's first victim) is represented here by Elizabeth Bell; John Lowe (the pastor whom Hopkins had hanged a witch) here becomes John Knowles; and so on. The poem is indebted to *Witches and Neighbours: the Social and Cultural Context of European Witchcraft* by Robin Briggs, *Witchfinders: a Seventeenth-century English Tragedy* by Malcolm Gaskill, *The Witch-hunt in Early Modern Europe* by Brian P. Levack, and *Witch Hunters: Professional Prickers, Unwitchers and Witch Finders of the Renaissance* by P.G. Maxwell-Stuart. The speaker conflates and misquotes Biblical passages from Psalms 19:1 and 19:5, and John 3:29. The closing lines of the poem recall an image in a letter from Rainer Maria Rilke to his wife Clara, 9 July 1904; though how the narrator managed to do this is frankly beyond me.

The Footnote

A true story. The incident described in the poem is mentioned in, among other places, Michael Braddick's *God's Fury, England's Fire: a New History of the English Civil Wars.*

The Curlew

As the poem indicates, the words attributed to George Fox (1624-91) are adapted from entries in his journal: see George Fox, *The Journal,* ed. Nigel Smith (Penguin, 1998) pp.13-35. That the Quakers "would not come into no great towns, but lived in the fells like butterflies" was an accusation made by Thomas Ledgerd, an alderman of Newcastle upon Tyne. Fox proved him wrong by visiting the city in 1658 and challenging him to an open debate: when Ledgerd declined, Fox asked "Who was the butterflies now?" (p.254). Fox claimed that when he was an eight-year-old boy he was visited by God: "Be as a stranger unto all" was His command.

scumfish: stuffy, stale (pron. *scumf*-ish)

Brantwood Senilia

The speaker is John Ruskin (1819-1900), and many lines and images in the poem have been adapted freely from his writings. See *The Works of John Ruskin,* edited by E.T. Cook and A. Wedderburn, Vol. II p.34; IV p.86, p.148; XII p.311; XXIII p.22, p.36, p.306-08, p.334; XXV p.13, p.63, p.232, p.238, pp.245-46; XXVII p.70, p.127, pp.130-31, pp.335-36; XXIX pp.30-31, pp.37-38, p.175, p.382, p.385, pp.392-93; XXXV pp.132-33; XXXVI p.504; and XXXVII p.107, p.117, p.156. I also made use of a phrase from an unpublished letter by Ruskin to his sister Joan, which is quoted on p.246 of the second volume of Tim Hilton's excellent biography.

"My dear little birds…": Ruskin wrote many letters to the girls at Winnington Hall School, to be read out to them by their teacher, and this is how he usually addressed the girls.

The five stanzas beginning "Up my spirit leapt, so glad…" are a translation of the second section of the anonymous medieval poem *Pearl*, though, as far as I know, there is no evidence that Ruskin ever read it. Ruskin translated the inscription at the foot of the sepulchral slab in Santa Croce as follows: "This Galileo of the Galilei was, in his times, the head of philosophy and medicine; who also in the highest magistracy loved the republic marvellously; whose son, blessed in inheritance of his holy memory and well-passed and pious life, appointed this tomb for his father, for himself, and for his posterity." Compare the epitaph Ruskin wrote for his own father: "He was an entirely honest merchant, and his memory is, to all who keep it, dear and helpful. His son, whom he loved to the uttermost and taught to speak truth, says this of him." The line that begins "…came Phaedra then, and Procris", and the ten that follow it, are freely translated from the *Odyssey*, XI, 321-25. *insanae substructiones*: mad structures; *inutiles domos*: useless buildings; *Inibito a chiunque il vendere frutti cattivi*: it is forbidden to sell rotten fruit; *cujus sancte memorie*: in whose holy memory; "we have a little sister, and she has no breasts: what shall we do for our sister in the day of her espousals?" is from the Song of Solomon 8:8, but the phrasing is Ruskin's; *concessum propter duritiem cordis*: a concession made on account of the hardness of men's hearts (Matthew 19:8); "O, feed her with apricocks & dewberries, / with purple grapes, green figs & mulberries" is misremembered from *A Midsummer Night's Dream*, III, i, 8-89.

The Marble Veil
'The Gospel of St Thomas' (trans. Marvin Meyer) is quoted in parts II, V, VI, and VII. Other quotations: I: *al cielo e al tempo*: to heaven and to time (Giosuè Carducci, 'Dinanzi alle Terme di Caracalla'); III: *il lampo che candisce / alberi e muri e*

li sorprende in quella / eternità d'istante [...] / strana sorella: the lightning that bleaches trees and walls and astonishes them in that eternal instant [...] strange sister (Eugenio Montale, 'La bufera'); IV: 'The Aspern Papers', Henry James; VI: *A le cineree trecce alzato il velo verde*: the green veil was lifted up to the grey braided hair (Carducci, as above); VII: *Introduction to the Devout Life* (Part Three, Chapter Three), St. Francis de Sales; 'On the Extinction of the Venetian Republic', William Wordsworth; *The Stones of Venice*, John Ruskin; *Antony and Cleopatra*, II.v.29, William Shakespeare; VIII: Rilke's letter to the Princess Marie von Thurn und Taxis-Hohenlohe, 23 July 1920; *"Censimento" dei Rom e controllo dei soldi pubblici spesi*: "census" of Roma and control of public spending (tweeted by Matteo Salvini on 19 June 2018); *wie eine Nymphe die den Zeus empfing*: like a nymph who received Zeus (Rainer Maria Rilke, 'Venezianischer Morgen' — part VIII also ends with two lines that are my free translation of the closing lines of this poem); IX: *veler*: a maker of ships' sails.